The Bargaining for Israel

In the Shadow of Armageddon

Mona Johnian

BRIDGE-LOGOS *Publishers*

North Brunswick, New Jersey

The Scriptures quoted in this book are taken from the following four versions of the Bible: *The Jewish New Testament,* the Tenakh, The New King James Version, and the King James Version.

The Bargaining for Israel: In the Shadow of Armageddon
by Mona Johnian
ISBN: 0-88270-698-5
Library of Congress Catalog Card Number: 96-85170
Copyright © 1996 by Mona Johnian

Published by:
BRIDGE-LOGOS *Publishers*
North Brunswick Corporate Center
1300 Airport Road, Suite E
North Brunswick, NJ 08902

"'Bibi,' King of Israel!" the crowd cheered.

With the cameras of the world looking on, and Orthodox Jews dancing in the streets, Benjamin "Bibi" Netanyahu became the prime minister of Israel, as this book was going to press.

Educated at a citadel of intelligentsia, strong conservative ideologue Benjamin Netanyahu took a degree in architecture at the Massachusetts Institute of Technology in Boston. But the drawing board of Middle Eastern politics is a far cry from a classroom. How Netanyahu will take the divided building blocks of his nation and pull them together with the international community remains to be seen—and is certain to give him a place in history, for honor or dishonor.

"Anxious World Waits as a New Leader Emerges," was the caption on the front page of "USA Today." But more than a new leader is emerging in Israel. The age old desire for a king is brewing in the cup. Such words as "theocracy" (God administered government) is being written into the daily news. Undivided Jerusalem has been promise, perhaps even as undivided Israel. As one Palestinian observed, "The people of Israel have forgotten the 'peace' Now they elect the war." (2A Mon. June 3rd, 1996 USA Today)

"The war?"
What war? Is the shadow of Armageddon beginning to emerge over a fragile world peace? Has a Goliath arrived on the scene? Even more so, has a David finally emerge to settle the issues? The next few years will answer all these questions. The next few pages will help us to understand the answers.

i

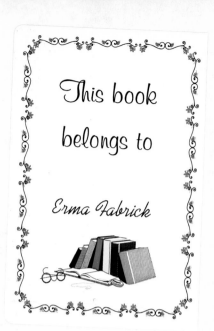

This book

belongs to

Erma Fabrick

Table of Contents

Introduction   The New Millennium vii
Chapter   1   Seven Reasons Why Nations Fail . 1
Chapter   2   Dividing Israel for Peace or War? 29
Chapter   3   Israel's Defender 35
Chapter   4   Securing Israel's Borders 41
Chapter   5   The Spirit Behind World Powers 45
Chapter   6   War Is Coming 51
Chapter   7   Two Great Waves of Power 61
Chapter   8   The Profile of the Antichrist 75
Chapter   9   The Marriage Supper 91
Chapter 10   Parable of the Ten Virgins 103
Chapter 11   The Restoration of All Things 117
Chapter 12   Who Will Rule the World? 125
Chapter 13   A Signal From Russia 141
Chapter 14   The Last Hour 155
Chapter 15   Elijah Is Coming 167

Introduction

The New Millenium

The next ten years may be the most important of your life. I base this on the fact that you and I belong to the generation that will greet a brand-new millennium.

As the twentieth century becomes a part of history, we are seeing the consummate experience of 6,000 years since Adam coming to a head. Millennium number seven has arrived. Is January 1, 2000, a mystical day? Probably not—but life on planet earth is slated for dramatic changes in the years ahead. How do we know this?

Because this present millennium (number six) is witnessing the death of this world's system. Because God has engineered radical changes in each millennium since recorded history.

Consider the record:

In Millennium #1, God announced His plan to make the earth habitable. Adam was created. Adam sinned. God pronounced judgment on man.

In Millennium #2, Noah and the Deluge came. God pronounced judgment on the earth. The first time by flood; the next time by fire.

In Millennium #3, (2,000 to 1,000 B.C.), three great pronouncements were made:

a. God called a man named Abraham and through him made an eternal covenant with man. He then established the national boundaries of Abraham's descendants in the Middle East.

b. God called Moses and gave Abraham's descendants the land of Israel.

c. God called David and confirmed that same land as David's kingdom forever.

In Millennium #4, (1,000 B.C. to 3 A.D., and the birth of Jesus). Jesus as a descendant of the royal house of David qualified for His eternal throne. He also ratified in blood God's legal rights to govern the nations and all creation.

In Millennium #5, (From the Resurrection of Christ to 1,000 A.D.) The Church was birthed and the Kingdom of Heaven was made available to all nations through faith in Jesus.

In Millennium #6, (1,000 A.D. to the present time) The program of God has continued to advance by the Holy Spirit in the Church. Sin in the world system has ripened and come to fruition. The cup of iniquity which God watches over is full. The nations now qualify to be judged:

> Then I looked, and behold, a white cloud, and on the cloud sat One like the Son of Man, having on His head a golden crown, and in His hand a sharp sickle. And another angel came out of the temple, crying

with a loud voice to Him who sat on the cloud,
"Thrust in Your sickle and reap, for the time has come
for You to reap, for the harvest of the earth is ripe."
(Revelation 14:14, NKJV)

In Millennium #7 (2000 A.D. -), with ample
confirmations from the Scriptures, which we shall point
out in this book, we may well expect the coming of the
Son of God to establish the Kingdom of Heaven upon the
earth for the 1,000 years of restoration. Then mankind will
go back into eternity where it all began.

The Sum Total

In the beginning God created—in the end He will
judge—in the Millennium He will restore—in eternity He
will reign in full glory. This is the sum total of
world history.

The head of Trends Research Institute was quoted in
the *Boston Globe,* September, 1993, as saying, "All
systems worldwide are breaking down, including ours"
(*Boston Globe,* September 13, 1993, p. 34, col. 3). The
revolutions of the past have now become the convulsions
of a terminally ill world system. The ancient principalities
and powers of the Middle East are stirring themselves up
to gain dominion. The last bargaining chips for power are
falling on the table of human government. The question
of David's kingdom keeps pushing its way to the top of
the list. Man's day is drawing to a close; the Lord's day
is about to begin.

The Ultimate Challenge

In 1963, King Hussein of Jordan completed the
restoration of the ceiling of the Dome of the Rock. This
gilded dome of Islamic significance contains 45,000

golden mosaic tiles, some of which are inscribed with verses from the Koran. For artistic beauty and craftsmanship, the dome deserves to be seen by every human eye. For both spiritual and political aggression, the dome should be seen by every spiritual eye as the ultimate challenge concerning who will rule the world—Christ or Antichrist? Whoever rules the temple mount in Jerusalem, will ultimately rule the world. The Jewish prophets declared, *And the Lord shall inherit Judah his portion in the holy land, and shall choose Jerusalem again* (Zechariah 2:12). But the Islamic dome which sits over the ancient sight of Israel's first temple has written on the outside of its golden face, "God has no Son."

If someone invades the land you bought and calls it his own and he sits down at your table and convincingly declares that you do not exist, wouldn't you call it the ultimate challenge? Muhammad not only disannuled the deity of Jesus as Messiah, but his legacy has claimed the sacred temple mount for Allah. What is more, traditionally, the non-Islamic world has bought into the belief that Allah is one and the same as the God of Israel and the Church.

With the rise of Islam in America and the West, thinking people have begun to ask the question, *Who is Allah and what is this new religion called Islam?* In 1996, Hillary Clinton, the First Lady of the United States of America, made a pilgrimage to Turkey. Standing inside a mosque, she made an official declaration for a second time that, "What the world needs is more religious tolerance." But to speak of religious tolerance in the religious citadel of religious intolerance is ironic. It is somewhat like standing inside a prison surrounded by criminals and preaching law and order to the outside world. The overwhelming evidence of history shows that the god Muhammad met has tolerance only for Allah.

Who Is Allah?

Using numerous references, author Ramon Bennett writes, "The roots of Islam are buried in Arabia—in Mecca—in a square stone building called the Ka'abah. ...In the Ka'abah, there were 350 *ginn* (genies—idols, angels, and demons), one of whom was called Allah."

"Allah is a pre-Islamic name ...corresponding to the Babylonian Bel."

"Allah-worship, as well as the worship of Baal, were both astral religious in that they involved the worship of the sun, the moon, and the stars."

"In Arabia, the sun-god was viewed as a female goddess and the moon as the male god. ...The name Allah was used as the personal name of the moon god." (*Philistine*, by Ramon Bennett, pg. 46, 47).

Every mosque today has the symbol of the crescent moon on it—the ancient symbol of Allah, the moon-god. It is this Allah that is saying to the world today, "Allah—not the Son of the God of Israel—rules the temple mount in Jerusalem." It is the same sacred site that God promised King David's heirs forever.

When Gabriel appeared to Mary, to announce the birth of Jesus, he said of Jesus, "*He will be great, and will be called the Son of the Highest; and the Lord God will give Him the throne of His father David. And He will reign over the house of Jacob forever, and of His kingdom there will be no end*" (Luke 1:32-33, NKJV).

It's Hard to Swallow

It's hard to swallow the Islamic teaching about Allah, when you read that he was first worshiped as one of 360 deities in Arabia. It's hard to swallow the claims of Muhammad when you realize he was not of the royal line of David. It's hard to swallow a mosque that rests on the one spot that God declared is the temple site of His Son. (See Psalm 2.) It is impossible to swallow Islam as the law that will go forth from the Temple Mount to govern all nations.

> *In the days to come, the Mount of the Lord's House shall stand firm above the mountains and tower above the hills; and all the nations shall gaze on it with joy. And the many peoples shall go and say: "Come, let us go up to the Mount of the Lord, to the House of the God of Jacob; that He may instruct us in His ways, and that we may walk in His paths." For instruction shall come forth from Zion, the word of the Lord from Jerusalem. Thus He will judge among the nations and arbitrate for the many peoples....*
> (Isaiah 2:2-4a, Tanakh)

According to Islam, the law of Muhammad will one day go out of Mecca and from the Temple Mount and cover the entire earth. One of the mandates of the late Ayatollah Khomieni was that every home will fly the flag of Islam.

But according to the Bible, the Law of the Lord for the nations will go out of Jerusalem from the Temple Mount. Enthroned on that mount as Sovereign over the nations will be Jesus.

> *...Thus speaketh the Lord of hosts, saying, Behold the man whose name is The BRANCH; and he shall*

> *grow up out of his place, and he shall build the temple of the Lord; Even he shall build the temple of the Lord; and he shall bear the glory, and shall sit and rule upon his throne; and he shall be a priest upon his throne: and the counsel of peace shall be between them both.* (Zechariah 6:12-13)

The Question of the Temple Site

The question the present international peace-keeping community needs to ask is, *Who will retain the temple site. Allah or Jehovah God of Israel?* Peace will not exist in the Middle East, or anywhere in the world, until that question is answered to God's satisfaction. And we can easily understand God's satisfaction if we glance back approximately 3,000 years to the city of Jerusalem when King David had a visit from an angel of the Lord.

Contrary to God's orders, David assessed the numerical strength of his army one day, causing judgment to fall on Israel, and 70,000 men died. An angel was then sent to Jerusalem to destroy it, but just as the sword of destruction was about to fall, the Lord stayed his hand. At the moment he was stopped, the angel was standing by a threshing floor that belonged to a man named Ornan. In an open vision, David saw the angel standing between heaven and earth with a drawn sword. He and the elders of Israel covered themselves with sackcloth and literally threw their bodies face-down on the ground, pleading for mercy.

What the angel instructed David to do next settles the question of the temple site forever. Upon instruction, David rushed to Ornan, bought the threshing floor, built an altar, and sacrificed a burnt offering. God answered him with fire from heaven and ordered the angel to return his sword to his sheath.

Moved by God's great mercy David declared that, *Here will be the House of the Lord and here the altar of burnt offerings for Israel* (1 Chronicles 22:1).

From that day until his death, David began to collect materials for the Temple of the Lord that would be built in Jerusalem. *"Then David gave Solomon the blueprint of the Temple and its surroundings....For the Holy Spirit had given David all these plans"* (1 Chronicles 28:11-12, TLB) and the question of the Temple Mount was forever settled.

Contrary to the Koran of Islam, the God of Israel selected the site of the Temple Mount for Himself. Where the golden face now sits and declares that this God has no Son, Isaiah proclaimed, *"...a child has been born to us, a son has been given us. And authority has settled on his shoulders...upon David's throne and kingdom, that it may be firmly established...now and forever. The zeal of the Lord of Hosts shall bring this to pass"* (Isaiah 9:5-6).

The Temple Mount is *spiritual.* Worldwide worship will be offered to the one who sits enthroned there. The Temple Mount is *political.* All nations will follow the law that comes from its governor.

War is brewing. The site of the Battle of Armaggedon is approximately fifty-seven miles down the road from the Temple site. All nations will be involved before it is over.

Mankind's response to worship and government has been his downfall. His nature is lawless; and his spirit is blinded by mental reasoning, as we shall see in the next chapter, "Seven Reasons Why Nations Fail."

1

Seven Reasons Why Nations Fail

The problem of Adam and Eve was not lack of faith in the existence of God. They knew that He existed; He called on them regularly. Their problem was government. Human nature has a problem with government. It refuses to accept the idea that some things are off-limits, even deadly. Human intellect has equal difficulty accepting the idea of an intelligence that is higher than its own.

In a universe replete with absolute evidence of numerous levels of intelligence, from insect to man, we somehow refuse to believe in a God of highest intelligence. In a universe that man knows full well he did not create, he would rather say the universe created itself than to admit to a Governor with intelligence enough to do it on His own.

To acknowledge a Creator-Governor would be to acknowledge His right to establish policy, and human government would consequently be required to submit to a higher authority—which for 6,000 years it has refused to do. In order to deal with end-time events, we must realize that we are talking about the final conflict of two opposing governments—human and divine.

1

The evidence speaks for itself. Human history has failed. Given time, human beings pollute everything they touch. In this chapter, we are going to take a brief look at seven reasons why this happens.

According to the Bible, various nations, languages, and religions developed over the earth as a result of the moral, religious, and political corruption at Babylon, where civilization had its second beginning. Because of evil, the human race had been virtually destroyed by a worldwide flood, which drowned all but eight people. Yet, approximately 100 years later, we find that mankind had readopted its same old rebellious ways, and under the leadership of one of Noah's great grandsons, Nimrod, the human race was once again in religious, moral, and political decay. Since that time, the name "Babylon" has been used to describe nations that rebel against God.

In reality, the system at Babylon was a literal, spiritual program planned by Satan for the destruction of nations. It is the same plan he uses from generation to generation.

I watched a documentary one evening on Marco Polo's travels to the Far East. At one point he encountered a mystic who purported to have discovered the secret to eternal life through earth, wind, and fire. I said to my family, "Can you believe that is the same lie many people still believe today?" Then the Holy Spirit spoke back to me, *Yes, because the devil only has to deceive one generation at a time*!

National failure is the price for adopting the Babylonian system of religious, moral, and political rebellion.

Human nature and God's nature remain the same from generation to generation. Styles may and do change, but the ground rules for social behavior are intransigent. Whatever God blessed in the past, He blesses today. Whatever He judged and condemned in the past, He judges and condemns today. Let us look now at reason number one for national failure.

Reason #1: Pride

The first cause for national failure we want to consider on divine history's fatality list is pride.

> Call together the archers against Babylon: all ye that bend the bow, camp against it round about; let none thereof escape: recompense her according to her work; according to all that she hath done, do unto her: for she hath been proud against the Lord, against the Holy One of Israel (Jeremiah 50:29).

Isaiah talks about, "The burden of Babylon, which Isaiah the son of Amoz did see ...I will cause the arrogancy of the proud to cease, and will lay low the haughtiness of the terrible" (Isaiah 13:1-11).

The great national leader, King Solomon, said: "When pride cometh, then cometh shame" (Proverbs 11:2). He also said, "Pride goeth before destruction, and an haughty spirit before a fall" (Proverbs 16:18).

National respect is healthy. I am honored to be an American. I think my country is tops on this earth. In every country where I travel I find people who are proud to be German, Polish, English, Greek, and so forth. But national pride that ignores the laws of God is deadly. Any nation, that loses its reverence for God, however great its culture, is destined for destruction.

Recently, a man from the utility company came to our home for the monthly meter reading. My husband Paul took it as an opportunity to bless him with some good news. The man responded, "Look, sir, I don't want to be disrespectful, but I'm not interested in hearing about God. I am going to hell. That's where I want to go. So please do not talk to me about it!"

You could call that response hard and insensitive, but it was laced with bits of reverence here and there. Allow me to

3

cite another case that expresses the blatant American arrogance we see growing like a disease in this and other western nations today. Paul walked into an establishment to say hello to a man we had not seen for several years.

"Hello, Paul, how are things going with you?" the man inquired.

"Simply great, Mr. Strong! I just came back from Russia!"

"What were you doing in Russia—playing the violin?"

"Yes, I played the violin," Paul said. "But more than that, I was preaching the gospel!"

Like a flash, Mr. Strong retorted, "Well, I hope you didn't come in here to preach, because if you did, I'm not interested!"

It is one thing to sin and be quiet about it; it is another to flaunt our sins in God's face. It is one thing to question the reality of God; it is another to challenge Him. It is one thing to reject a Christian's witness; it is another to scorn the content.

Paul wrote to Timothy: "This know also, that in the last days perilous times shall come. For men shall be lovers of their own selves, covetous, boasters, proud, blasphemers, disobedient to parents, unthankful, unholy, Without natural affection, truce-breakers, false accusers, incontinent, fierce, despisers of those that are good, Traitors, heady, highminded, lovers of pleasures more than lovers of God" (2 Timothy 3:1-4).

Another young man came to our home one day to do some work based on a contract. Because I witnessed to him, his boss called two days later in a heat of anger saying, "We are not fulfilling our contract with you unless your wife keeps her mouth shut!"

4

"Hold it!" Paul said in an equally loud voice. "You are not going to tell us what we can and cannot say in our own home! We still have freedom of speech in this country! We are ministers of the gospel and we speak by the prompting of God, not man!"

"I'm calling the Attorney General's office!" the man retorted, and hung up. About an hour later the man called back and said, "Well, we are going to finish the contract, but we don't want any talking."

"What you do about this contract is up to you," Paul said, "but I am not going to promise you anything!" We knew he was legally bound to finish the job, of course, because we also called the Attorney General!

This incident is repeated many times a day in America—the land of good people and churches. The devil is bold. He speaks ever so authoritatively through proud, boastful people. America has changed drastically!

I grew up in rural America. Certainly not everyone in our small world was a committed Christian. Some were even downright heathen. But only two men were ever known to curse God, and their godless conduct was like leprosy to the rest of the community, because people had a fear of God. Even when they did not serve Him, they respected those who did. Ministers were called "Reverend," and apologies were made for profane words spoken "out of order."

What we find now is bold vulgarity—children swearing at parents, women swearing at men, men swearing from the pulpit. Before we went into the ministry, our former pastor used profanity in his sermons. Just this week we were cursed loudly in the streets by three other drivers.

In our many years of trying to witness in the marketplace of the great city of Boston, the typical response we get from people is either one of anger or "Look, that's fine for you but

I don't need it!" Do you know why people feel they do not need God? Because they have been led to believe there are no absolutes. Under the influence of modern humanism, which deifies man, and mechanistic science, which deifies matter, man has become uncertain about everything except his own arrogance. We would do well to remember that the ancient empire of Greece began to decline after its great philosophers and playwrights stripped the people of all absolutes through mental reasonings. It is past time for America and the international community to wake up, get off their intellectual high horse and come back down to reality.

There *are* absolutes in life. A trip to the funeral home confirms this fact. A flight on an airplane confirms this fact. A trip to a maternity ward confirms this fact. And since there are undeniable absolutes in this world, who is to say that God does not exist? Have you ever wondered who decided to call a spiritually ignorant person an intellectual just because he or she has technological knowledge? Yet, we think nothing of calling a highly educated spiritual person ignorant!

I loved it some years back when an opera star provided complete television coverage of a presidential inaugural address with the old Quaker lyrics:

> 'Tis a gift to be simple, 'Tis a gift to be free;
> 'Tis a gift to come down to the place you ought to be.
> And when you find yourself in the place just right,
> You'll be in the valley of love and delight.

Pride is the first step toward national failure.

Reason #2: Hedonism
The second cause for national failure on divine history's casualty list is hedonism: living for pleasure through spiritual and moral assassination.

Babylon, Greece, and Rome were three great world empires. Yet look at what occupied their time before they fell into a dusty history: food orgies, sexual orgies, sports and theater orgies, and mind orgies. Rome, once a great empire, became so obsessed with sports extravaganzas that they went from watching gladiators kill each other to watching hungry lions eat Christians. Then just to see the blood flow, they began to put horses in the arena for slaughter. The Caesars actually thought of themselves as gods.

> Therefore hear now this, thou that art given to pleasures, that dwellest carelessly, that sayest in thine heart, I am, and none else beside me; I shall not sit as a widow, neither shall I know the loss of children: ...For thou hast trusted in thy wickedness: thou hast said, None seeth me. Thy wisdom and thy knowledge, it hath perverted thee; and thou hast said in thine heart, I am, and none else beside me. Therefore shall evil come upon thee; thou shalt not know from whence it riseth: and mischief shall fall upon thee; thou shalt not be able to put it off: and desolation shall come upon thee suddenly, which thou shalt not know. (Isaiah 47:8-11)

The word "mischief" in Isaiah's warning means ruin. God says people who devote their time to physical pleasures and self-serving goals will have mischief fall upon their circumstances before they know it. Trouble will come from unexpected directions and their lives will come crashing down around them.

Just before the nation of Israel fell at one point in their history, Judges 17:6 records of them, "Every man did that which was right in his own eyes." Today we call this "personal choice."

I watched a medical doctor's report on the crises the world faces because of the pandemic spread of sexually transmitted diseases. "We simply can no longer afford our careless life-style," she said. God gave us this warning hundreds of years earlier; He said that no nation can afford a morally careless, pleasure-mad mentality.

One thing that is feeding today's sexual insanities is the music industry. Rock music has now reached a point of such decadence that mothers have gone all the way to Congress seeking help. Filthy lyrics, sensuous rhythms, performers who only vaguely resemble members of the human race have hypnotized the whole earth. Nobody can escape their tormenting noise, because it blares in the majority of public places. Many times I am filled with humiliation as I shop in department stores with strangers of all ages while loud, vulgar rhythms and lyrics suggest we are all in a flophouse. Careless music encourages careless living, and together they spell ruin.

The spirit of Rome is not far from any nation when a single sports figure can command a million or more dollars a year for playing a game. When statistics show that 70,000,000 people take drugs in America today, and another 30,000,000 are on alcohol—which means almost every other person is stoned—pleasure madness is not far from us.

Half-stoned people fill stadiums all over the world. They scream and yell, and some riot and murder, because we have become a generation intoxicated with pleasure. Pleasure has become a multi-billion-dollar-a-year industry.

It all sounds so wholesome to say, "My child is interested in sports." But one evening during the summer, Paul and I stopped by the ballfield with our son to watch the ending of a game between two local teams. The yelling, swearing, and frenzy of the parents was frightening as the game drew to a close. Angry fists waved threats back and forth, until one boy finally managed the winning score. As that last run was coming in, shouts went up in one great thunder. Yet, Christians who clap their hands or wave their arms in an anthem of praise to the God who gives us our very life are called radical!

Some athletes take steroids to build up muscle tissue. Some take other drugs to provide them with an extra "boost." Small-time bets and big-time gamblers risk paychecks on the would-be winners. Joggers, fitness clinics, public school programs, worldwide competitions, and Super Bowls—we are a generation "given" to physical activities.

No one questions that, in perspective, clean sports and physical activity have their place in life. But America left "cow pasture" athletics and wholesome pleasure forty years ago. Today's fitness and sports mania is nothing more than clever corporate manipulation.

We are a nation that worships a "golden calf." The human body and sports activities have become a number-one priority to many. God gave us the balance between the body and the spirit when He said, "Bodily exercise profiteth little: but godliness is profitable unto all things, having promise of the life that now is, and of that which is to come" (1 Timothy 4:8). Every time I see a jogger, I want to remind him or her that godliness will do more for his or her health than running will.

When the public school system of the United States makes physical education a law, while at the same time declaring that any mention of biblical realities is illegal and harmful to our children, I want to cry out, "Wake up, America! You have a new idol. You have become a nation of flesh worshipers!" The fall of ancient Rome echoes this warning. There is more to life than great colosseums.

How is it that great civilizations begin with such noble aims, only to end upon their knees before the passions of the flesh? What causes us to be repeatedly reduced to frivolous living? I believe the answer lies in our third reason for national failure.

Reason #3: Idol Worship

One of God's first laws to mankind concerned the worship of idols. In the Book of Exodus, God warns, "Thou shalt not make unto thee any graven image, or any likeness of any thing that is in heaven above, or that is in the earth beneath, or that is in the water under the earth" (Exodus 20:4-5).

No knee should ever bow before any human being, nor anything created by the hands of a mere person. Whether it be Christian or pagan in title or subject matter, no man deserves the praise that belongs only to God.

Ignorant worship is a major cause for natural failure. Ignorant worship is worship of any person or man-made object other than Yahweh, that is, God and His Son, Christ Jesus.

Jeremiah says, "Therefore, behold, the days come, that I will do judgment upon the graven images of Babylon: and her whole land shall be confounded, and all her slain shall fall in the midst of her" (Jeremiah 51:47).

War and confusion always plague a land that delves into idol worship, and all the world falls into this category in one way or another. Stop and think of how God must feel when He looks at the human race and sees most of its people on their knees before a piece of wood or stone or some personality that men have appointed to office.

Almost half of the world's population worships visible, hand-created idols. This means that on any given day, approximately two billion people bow down and ask a dead god to hear their hearts' cries. The other half of the human race is consumed with a different kind of idolatry, but one that is just as real, as they bow before the passions and pleasure-hungers of their human nature.

How sad and how thoroughly disgusting that after 6,000 years of prophets, martyrs, Scriptures, and ministers, people still prefer their idols to the truth!

10

How is it possible? Let's go back to the Book of Isaiah and read again:

> Therefore hear this now, you who are given to pleasures, who dwell securely, who say in your heart, "I am, and there is no one else besides me; I shall not sit as a widow, Nor shall I know the loss of children"; ...For you have trusted in your wickedness; You have said, "no one sees me;" Your wisdom and your knowledge have warped you; And you have said in your heart, "I am, and there is no one else besides me." (Isaiah 47:8-10, NKJV)

Why can a nation go to ruin? How are they deceived into a false sense of security? They are blinded by their wisdom and their knowledge. Human wisdom and knowledge were the idols that led ancient Israel to ruination. They looked to their carnality to set their standards and solve their problems. The same error is being repeated again today. In the past fifty years, secular humanists have systematically redesigned the philosophy of the entire western world into a spiritually careless mentality. Through a process of psychological labeling we have categorized and dignified every base behavior of humankind. Using medical terminology, we have excused and justified every unchecked desire of the most primitive urges until guilt no longer exists.

Rich in explanations but short on solutions, we in the United States have finally arrived at a time when we no longer know what to do with our lawbreakers and hardened criminals. According to government criminologists, we are headed for a decade of "superpredators." These are children between the ages of nine and twelve who will murder and rob for the thrill of it, with no sense of remorse—and nobody can stop it."

God says, "Let no man deceive himself. If any man among you seemeth to be wise in this world, let him become a fool, that he may be wise. For the wisdom of this world is foolishness with God" (1 Corinthians 3:18-19). "For it is written, I will destroy the wisdom of the wise, and will bring to nothing the understanding of the prudent" (1 Corinthinans 1:19).

Running to the "experts" no longer works. According to former President George Bush, the number-one threat facing the world today is nuclear proliferation among developing nations. He cited the second great threat as "uncertainty." Are we any closer to solving the devastation of world hunger? Not even with millions of dollars. We conquer one problem only to have four threats break out in another location. But the Bible tells us, "The Lord knoweth the thoughts of the wise, that they are vain. Therefore let no man glory in men" (1 Corinthians 3:20-21).

Education will never solve the important issues of our day in and of itself. Its contribution to humanity is the dispensation of information. It takes wisdom of spirit to use our information constructively. We need to stop worshiping the experts and go back to the Book that contains the real answers.

Mind-worship is idolatry.

After Paul and I met Jesus in full commitment, one of the first things God did in our home was to set us free from our dead idols. This meant that some of what we had called "fine art" had to be laid to rest in the bottom of our dirty, beat-up garbage can. God showed us that pagan idols are not works of art—but they are clever power objects of the devil. Take a look at any nation that is steeped in idol worship and, given time, see if they do not become a plagued people. "Neither shalt thou bring an abomination into thine house, lest thou be a cursed thing like it: but thou shalt utterly detest it, and thou shall utterly abhor it; for it is a cursed thing" (Deuteronomy 7:26).

The next thing Paul and I did, when we began to clear our home of idols, was to pull down the golden calf of *education*!

You may be thinking, "People have to be educated!"

Yes, but they do not have to worship and sacrifice their souls on its altar. For example, God said we are to train our children morning and evening, at mealtime and in bed, in the ways of God. But the average family does little or nothing to educate the *spirits* of their children. They are too busy driving them from kindergarten through college excellence, in hopes of giving them "the best."

The growing trend is no longer summer camps where young children go to swim, bike, and discover nature. We are now being encouraged to see that they are drilled at computer camps. It is another part of our obsessive wish to see how much knowledge we can cram into the minds of our young people. Never mind if their nervous systems cannot take it. Never mind if they are spiritual neophytes. For the sake of technology, cram and drill.

This generation has two categories of idols that are prevalent—the pleasures of the flesh and the achievements of the mind. But whether evil or admirable, an idol is anything that occupies the heart of a nation and causes it to turn from reverence and worship of the true and living God to worshiping the works of its own hands. America has turned. We are a nation intoxicated with our physical and mental idols.

In a Boston bookstore one evening, I became involved in a conversation with an intense young man. Giving me no chance to reply, he began reciting one-half hour of scientific data. The bookstore was about to close, so I finally interrupted his monologue. "What is your major in college?"

13

"Philosophy! After becoming bored with science and math I have found my niche in philosophy."

"Do you believe in God?" I questioned.

"No! I finally made up my mind three years ago that I am an atheist!" he said as though it were a badge of honor. "I'm happy!" he excitedly continued.

"I can see why," I responded wryly. "You've concluded that the funeral home is your destination. Extinction is a lot to be happy about."

"Oh, I'm not saying that I want to die," the man said.

"Then why do you consider death the logical conclusion to life?" I prodded.

"At death my cells are going to unite with the universe," he smiled. "I like to skydive, and recently when I jumped out of an airplane I was floating along with the birds." (By now the young man was moving his hands back and forth as if his arms were wings.) "And I felt at one with them!"

At one with the birds—at odds with God. It makes a lot of sense, doesn't it?

The Babylonian system is doing its work among us, and God is sending out the warning, *Western world, wake up! Throw out your pagan idols and return to the Book of wisdom that led you to your greatness.*

Reason #4: Immorality

This brings us to the fourth reason for national failure and the ever-increasing obsession in the western world called immorality. It is known as:

- The new morality, often involving "alternative life-styles."
- Personal sexual preferences.
- Adult maturity.
- Coming of age .
- Liberation, fun, pleasure, individual rights.

People call this phenomenon anything today but what it actually is—*immorality.*

Few people are sufficiently alarmed at the rampant disease of immorality that has swept the whole earth into an obsession with nocturnal delusions.

Each week we counsel a steady stream of all ages and both sexes whose lives are already totally devastated by the "new morality." Wealthy, poor, educated, uneducated, beautiful, ugly—no one is exempt from the wounds of today's unrestrained physical passions.

The morals of the United States and other western nations have collapsed so thoroughly that it is almost unbelievable to think there really was a time when a boy thought he had conquered the moon just by being able to kiss his girlfriend. The average definition of "virgin" today means a girl who has had only oral or hand-stimulated sex with her various male companions.

Almost 100 percent of today's television and movie plots presuppose all forms of sexual behavior from premarital and extramarital relationships to homosexual and bisexual partnerships. The subject of incest has already been introduced and will certainly gain acceptance on the screen, along with bestiality, just as surely as these expressions have gained widespread practice in the privacy of western homes. Numerous people of which we have personal knowledge, combined with a television report regarding an AIDS epidemic among cats in Huntsville, Alabama, tell us that many people are having sexual relationships with their dogs and cats.

"So what?" a belligerent young professional once challenged me. "What people do in the privacy of their homes is no one else's business!"

Fifty years ago I could have responded, "God says it is sin and will destroy a society." Today, I can still hold up

God's moral standard, but along with it I can give you the medical, psychological, and financial statistics that prove His words of warning to be accurate.

• Suicide is the second greatest cause of death today among teenagers. Liberated, and saturated, and spiritually uneducated, they get out the only way they know how.

• Oral sex has produced an incurable disease known as herpes that has exposed over 150 million Americans, with 250,000 new cases being discovered each year. Herpes is now considered by medical experts to be epidemic in its proportions.

• AIDS, a by-product of homosexual behavior initially, is still the most deadly incurable disease known to date. It has a one hundred percent mortality rate and continues to spread with all the vengeance of a plague. Add to this twenty other sexually transmitted diseases presently rampant on the earth and you will see that we have literally become a civilization crawling with communicable contamination.

Signs tell us, "Smoking is hazardous to your health." Where is the sign that says to young people, "Immorality may give you a deadly or incurable disease that will affect the rest of your life." Where are these AMA warnings about this?

Private immorality is a myth. We cannot even hide it from each other, much less God. Why do we think God warned us against such sexual lunacy? Because He wanted to deprive us of fun? No, God set up standards for human society because He knew the results of immorality would be physical and emotional devastation. He gave us these standards because He loves us.

Immorality destroys people, one at a time. People make up nations. Destroyed people become destroyed nations. It is simple arithmetic. If you study the great nations of the past, you will find that immorality was always present. Yet, it was when immorality became accepted and dignified as an alternate life-style that those societies began to decline.

I watched a special program on sex education in the public schools of America. After twenty-three years of special classes for our young people, the only definite findings reported were these:

1. Unwanted pregnancies decreased in schools that provided contraceptives without parental "interference"
2. Children now feel more comfortable about discussing sex in mixed company!

Those were the "positive" results. No one bothered to tabulate the negatives. What about the loss of our children's modesty and their sense of privacy and decency? Has the human race become so ignorant that we now need a professional to explain what insects and animals figure out on their own?

On one of our local television stations in Boston, two doctors held a Saturday morning forum for young grammar school children. We just happened to walk by when we heard these two adults explaining to our children every single detail of stimulation, ejaculation, and masturbation. They were taking calls city-wide from children wanting to know more. Needless to say, the station got a call from two adults at our house wanting to know more!

How dare those presumptuous professionals set themselves up as advisors to our children on a matter that involves not only the sanctity of the body but the very soul and spirit of our children.

Education tells us that it will not be evil if we stop calling it sin. That makes as much sense as saying, "Cancer will lose its power if we stop calling it a disease!"

I watched a Grammy award winner being interviewed one evening and was stunned to hear the young man say, "My wife is the only woman I have ever known. This is the way God planned it. And I feel great to be able to say to young people that I have had no desire to know any other woman than my wife!" What a beautiful testimony to God's system of morality.

Wake up, America! Wake up, western civilization! Wake up, eastern world! Stop dignifying, stop legalizing, stop practicing immorality, then God will heal our land. Why should we allow sin to destroy us? Immorality will cause a nation to fail. God says it. History proves it.

Reason #5: Sorceries and Drugs

In Revelation 18, we find God speaking to the world system concerning the philosophy that has deceived the nations throughout the centuries. He says to that system whose lifeline is fed by Satan, "...for by your sorceries were all nations deceived" (Reveleation 18:23).

Many parts of the world are totally consumed with occult practices, and no nation escapes their pollutions. In the past twenty years, America has gone from having citizens who were dabblers in the occult to having people who are devotees of occultism. What once seemed curious has become commonplace.

But witchcraft, astrology, hypnotism, fortune-telling, E.S.P., and Satan worship are actually only stepping-stones to an even greater move of worldwide dimensions. It is a plan explained in the Bible as "the great falling away." "Let no man deceive you by any means: for that day shall not come, except there come a falling away first" (2 Thessalonians 2:3).

What could possibly cross all religious and cultural barriers and actually effect changes in the religious attitudes of all nations? Sorcery. The definition of the word *sorcery* in the original Greek text is actually *pharmakeia*—drugs! Worldwide use of drugs has, is, and will continue to alter the thinking of men, women, and youths in every nation. What we need to understand is that drugs are not just a temporary alteration of thinking. A sizable number of the people we counsel at our center are people who have in some way been affected by drugs. We have learned through counseling that, short of a miracle, the drug-abused mind is permanently altered.

American statistics point to seventy million people in this nation who use drugs. Another thirty million are on alcohol. The number one problem in military discipline and combat readiness in the U. S. Armed Forces is drug use. From corporate executives to men in warehouses, almost half of the population in the United States is operating with altered thinking.

But drugs do not form the final stage of this master scheme. The Bible says, "By your sorceries [drugs] all nations were deceived" (Revelation 18:23).

Have you ever stopped to consider what great deception Satan is trying to bring about by altering the thinking of the entire human race? It is, of course, religious deception. Altered thinking is the devil's strategy for converting the thinking of the entire world from godly to satanic allegiance.

Actually, it is a plan that is quite easy to accomplish. When you realize that two-thirds of the world is already deceived by false gods, all that will be necessary to keep them quiet is to alter their moral objections to human persecution. Then Satan can move in on the Church for the kill. Even today what great defense could the church in America hope to receive within its own borders?

Stop and ask yourself—would the news media in America stand up for the rights of the Church if a severe attack were made against it? Would the legal profession come to its assistance? Would the Supreme Court rise up in its behalf? Would congress speak out?

When you stop to think about it, who but a conscience-seared society would outlaw prayer for children and legalize protection of immoral sexual deviants? Who in his clearest thinking would vote on whether to pass special laws protecting people based on the way they have sex? Modern sorcery causes the mind to lose its ability to determine future consequences of present decisions.

The fall of great civilizations does not occur overnight. It develops in proportion to wisdom's decline. Satan's plan to turn men from worship has been put in place. First, he drugged the world. Then he revived his age-old, man-centered worship. Shifting the eyes of mankind from God-consciousness to self-consciousness, Satan has deified the individual. It is not a new plan. As a matter of fact, it is very old and unoriginal.

Whittaker Chambers wrote,

> Humanism is not new. It is, in fact, man's second oldest faith. Its promise was whispered in the first days of the creation under the tree of the knowledge of good and evil: "Ye shall be as gods."

Self-realization—see it; obtain it. If you can dream it, you can have it. With unlimited powers of the mind, man is his own god. This is the basic philosophy that has charmed the fancy of the modern, egotistical human intellect.

The Apostle Paul described it this way: "If anyone teaches false doctrines and does not agree to the sound instruction of our Lord Jesus Christ and to godly teaching, he is *conceited* and understands nothing" (1 Timothy 6:3-4, NIV, italics added).

The world today is largely in the hands of conceited people who understand nothing, and they preside over populations whose thinking has been lulled into a chemical stupor. While we have slept and tripped out, conceited, humanistic educators have come in and removed God from our children. While we have played in and flooded the stadiums instead of the churches, stars and manger scenes have been replaced by fake genital body parts and prophylactics. While we rocked and rolled with people who look like scared chickens, every kind of filthy sexual practice conceivable has gained top-drawer legislative attention. Through sorcery—drug-altered psychology—the human race has prepared itself for massive spiritual deception.

Wake up, world! We are taking a prescription that is designed to produce social chaos. All humanistic, immoral, and occult psychology is birthed from direct demonic influence that is aimed at deceiving the nations. "For by thy sorceries were all nations deceived. And in her was found the blood of prophets, and of saints, and of all that were slain upon the earth" (Revelation 18:23-24).

Whenever satanic influence comes into a nation through occult practices, the spirit of murder is the next thing to follow. Remember, Jesus said Satan is here to " ...steal, and to kill, and to destroy" (John 10:10). One look at the abortion statistics and no one can deny that a spirit of murder has been released upon the whole earth today in a fresh way. This is what we are going to examine next—the sixth reason for national failure.

Reason #6: Martyrdom—Murder of the Innocents

Believers of every generation have been subjected to martyrdom. Our time is no different. The problem is that most Americans are unaware of it.

21

All present-day nations are involved in murder. Wherever ironclad communism still exists, people are martyred for their faith. Still others have chosen death for Christ, at the hands of fanatical Muslims, Hindus, tribal religions, and Buddhism. But aside from these religious convictions, every nation today is guilty of shedding innocent blood in a systematic, socially acceptable process called abortion. From God's vantage point, we are a bloody generation.

International abortion makes all other martyrdom pale in comparison. Every day in America alone, 41,000 unborn babies are slaughtered. People seem to have forgotten that, "...children are an heritage of the Lord: and the fruit of the womb is his reward" (Psalms 127:3).

Pharmaceutical companies have now produced genocidal drugs that will destroy life developed up to eight weeks with a simple pill. Women interviewed in a documentary about these pills spoke of abortion as though they were talking about a wart remover. With euphemistic, carefully chosen terminology, the host termed this approach to infanticide as a possible medical breakthrough which could eliminate "unwanted surgery."

Such a statement tells me that we are a generation that has gone mad on pleasures and personal power fantasies. How can mothers snuff out innocent lives that are separate individuals within our own host bodies, and hope to sleep at night? How can we bathe our nations in innocent blood and hope to escape the wrath of a holy God? How can we continue to rob God of His heritage and kid ourselves that He will not come looking for justice?

God is soon going to lift the skirts of every nation on this earth. He will be searching for the blood of innocent babies. For a woman to say, "I can do as I wish with my body" is spiritual arrogance, and for her to say, "I have a right to kill this life I am carrying in my body" is national suicide.

Anything that must be killed in order for it to be terminated is alive. That which develops into a human being begins as a person.

We have a beautiful grandson today because we refused the suggestion that he be terminated in the womb.

Reason #7: Oppression of Israel

Although it seems purely political, the seventh and final cause for national failure, oppression of Israel, is spiritual.

Dislike for Jewish people is a spiritual matter. Few people understand it, including Christians, yet no nation has ever willingly absorbed the Jews into their culture. More than anything else, Jews are tolerated as neighbors and dealt with in business because they cannot be squeezed out of the marketplaces. As for the land of Israel itself, the same spirit that hates the Jews hates the fact that they are in that particular spot of the earth.

This spiritual dislike for the nation of Israel is perfectly clear when you understand two of the promises God made to them. First of all, God put a mark of prosperity on the Jews that has baffled and irritated men of every generation of recorded history. In addition to giving them uncanny survivability, He promised them the land of His own private residence on earth—the land of Israel. Isaiah wrote:

> For the Lord will have mercy on Jacob, and will yet choose Israel, and set them in their own land: and the strangers shall be joined with them, and they shall cleave to the house of Jacob. ...Thou shalt take up this proverb against the king of Babylon, and say, How hath the oppressor ceased! the golden city ceased! (Isaiah 14:1-4)

23

Remember, Satan is the architect of the Babylonian system—the present-day world system—and he hates God's plans. Satan despises the fact that God is going to place His Messiah in control of the governments of this earth from the city of Jerusalem. This is why Satan puts hatred into all nations for Israel. Israel is the Messianic nation that has brought forth God's plan of judgment on Satan and his followers. He also knows that Jews are destined to inhabit that land by personal invitation of God. For this reason the land of Israel will continue to be harassed by the spiritually blinded Islamic worshipers until Jesus comes again.

Around 500 A.D., Satan revealed himself as an "angel of light" to a man named Muhammad in Saudi Arabia. He introduced "Allah" as the one true God. Then he sent out Muhammad across the Middle East to gain converts forcefully. Their movement came to be called "The Sword of Islam." Today Allah has approximately one billion worshipers called Muslims. Through their religious fervor, Satan continues to challenge God's plan by harassing His people and His property—Israel. This, briefly stated, is the primary root of the conflict in the Middle East, which will one day draw representatives of every nation on earth to the valley of Armageddon in an effort to seek resolution.

But in Genesis 17:19, God said to Abraham, "Sarah thy wife shall bear thee a son indeed; and thou shalt call his name Isaac: and I will establish my covenant with him for an everlasting covenant, and with his seed after him." Paul reiterated God's original intention when he wrote, "In Isaac shall thy seed be called" (Romans 9:7). In other words, the land of Israel and the descendants of Isaac have been called to the special mandate of hosting the Messiah. Not only did Isaac's descendants in the land of Israel bring forth the Messiah at His first coming, but they will also host him at His second coming.

24

Isaiah said of that day:

> Now it shall come to pass in the latter days That
> the mountain of the Lord's house Shall be established
> on the top of the mountains, And shall be exalted
> above the hills; And all nations shall flow to it. Many
> people shall come and say, "Come and let us go up
> to the mountain of the Lord, To the house of the God
> of Jacob; He will teach us His ways, And we shall
> walk in His paths." For out of Zion shall go forth the
> law, And the word of the Lord from Jerusalem. He
> shall judge between the nations, And shall rebuke
> many people; They shall beat their swords into
> plowshares, And their spears into pruning hooks;
> Nation shall not lift up sword against nation, Neither
> shall they learn war anymore. (Isaiah 2:2-4 NKJV)

Jesus came from the house of Jacob, and Jacob was
descended from Isaac. The land of Israel is deadly to any hand
that touches her, outside of the descendants of Isaac. This we
will discuss in more detail in later chapters.

Nations fail because human government does not work.
Human government does not work because it has the wrong
power behind it. This is what we want to look at next: The
Spirit Behind World Powers.

Although it seems purely political, the seventh and final
cause for national failure—the oppression of Israel—is
spiritual. Wars fought on earth originate in the heavenlies. The
apostle Paul made it clear that, "...we do not wrestle against
flesh and blood, but against principalities, against powers,
against spiritual hosts of wickedness in the heavenly places"
(Ephesians 6:12, NKJV).

Invisible to us, there is nevertheless a continual struggle between the Kingdom of God and the kingdom of Satan in the heavens. At the heart of their struggle is the question: Who will rule the world? Since God foreordained and has announced His plans to establish His Son upon the throne of world government, Satan has been forever attempting to overthrow this plan.

How does he do it? "The kings of the earth set themselves, and the rulers take counsel together, against the Lord, and against his anointed [Hebrew: *Mashiyach*—Messiah]" (Psalms 2:2). I will declare the decree: ...Thou are my Son; ...Ask of me, and I shall give thee the heathen for thine inheritance, and the uttermost parts of the earth for thy possession." (Psalm 2:7-8) Remember, what God decrees is a binding, legal command. It will absolutely be done. God has decreed that His Son will rule the governments of the earth. This point is vital in understanding the oppression of Israel and the never-ending struggles in the Middle East. God not only decreed His Son to rule, but He named the geographic location of His central headquarters as Zion. "Yet have I set my king upon my holy hill of Zion" (Psalms 2:6).

We human beings fail to appreciate the power and authority that God's Word carries. In the heavens they do understand. This is what has prompted all the wars of history and has birthed all the godless military leaders and political dictators. They are Satan's attempt to prevent the reign of God's Son, the Messiah.

From the divine point of view, the heart of this heavenly conflict has always been the Middle East for the obvious reason that God has selected Zion as the place of His Son's throne. Therefore, as the Scriptures repeatedly declare, Jerusalem will be the city of the last great conflict between God and Satan.

On May 8, 1948, Israel was declared a Jewish state and recognized by the United Nations. On July 30, 1980, Jerusalem was declared "eternal and indivisible" by the Israeli Parliament. Scripturally speaking, everything lines up for the Second Coming of Jesus and the final defeat of the antichrist at Armageddon, just outside the city of Jerusalem. This is looking at things from a biblical perspective. But what about the Islamic position? These "facts" to us become falsehoods from their perspective, and the destiny of the world is quite another picture to them.

In 570 A.D., Muhammad was born in Mecca (Saudi Arabia). His tribe, the Quraish, are supposed to have descended from Abraham through Ishmael. When he was forty years old, Muhammad began to receive revelations. Because he could neither read nor write, his knowledge depended on biblical information told to him by uninformed Christians in the declining Church of the Middle East and scanty Jewish understanding of the Scriptures. Muhammad's "revelations" mixed with faulty biblical knowledge to form his distorted, blasphemous dictations that were written down as the Koran.

As is repeatedly stated in the Koran, Muhammad ultimately came to believe that Adam, Abraham, Moses, and Jesus were prophets of God, but that he was the final prophet. It was Muhammad and his revelations that would usher in God's final kingdom on the earth. Muhammad taught that God had no son, that the Jews were rejected by God, that the Bible contains numerous errors, that Jesus did not die but ascended before His death, that Muhammad himself was Jesus' reference to the coming of the Holy Spirit. And finally that Zion is an Islamic holy place that will never be surrendered to Jewish or Christian infidels. Written in Arabic on the Gold Dome Mosque in Jerusalem are these words: " *God has no son.*"

All of this is in a direct contradiction to the entire Bible as Jews and Christians understand it. What it means is that Satan has planted a fanatically faithful people who will fight to the death upon the very spot God said His Son will reign. Two spirits working through the Jew and the Muslim demand the same spot of earth, and both are determined to fight to the death.

This is why no number of peace treaties signed here on earth hold any shred of hope. This battle is bigger than any and all peoples. This is why any nation that touches the land of Israel is doomed, because that property belongs to God's Son.

2

Dividing Israel for Peace or War?

Early in November of 1995, television viewers the world over stood speechless as a special bulletin announced that the Prime Minister of Israel, Yitzhak Rabin, had been shot. We were shocked for lack of understanding. Israel is an active volcano. Anyone who walks around her rim must measure every step, not by counselors from afar, but by the realities that exist from within her bubbling cauldron.

Israel's story is a completed manuscript. It has been written right down to the final eruption, and no amount of redactors can change even one line of the script. It is an epic that contains an heroic story called "David and Goliath."

The Original Intention

Goliath was a giant, and Israel has always had to contend with giants in her land. The giants are there in one form or another because the story of this mystical piece of property is bigger than people and their differences. There are two supernatural kingdoms struggling for this land of many names and many claims.

29

In reality, there is only one Author, one Owner, and one story of Israel's land and people. As important as every other nation is—and each one is important in its own right, true national importance is measured by each nation's relationship to Israel.

Jesus, quoting from the prophet Joel, clearly stated that when He returns all nations will be judged as nations based on their treatment of Israel.

> I will also gather all nations, and bring them down into the valley of Jehosphaphat, and will plead with them there for my people and for my heritage Israel, whom they have scattered among the nations, and parted my land. (Joel 3:2) (See also Matthew 25: 31-32, 40.)

Historically, the nations of the world have operated under a deception. They do not see the clear plan of God for the world, for the simple reason that they have chosen to believe a counterfeit scheme. One of the first things Jesus will do when He assumes full control of the earth is to bind Satan and freeze his deceptive influence over government. (See Revelation 20:3)

After 6,000 years of corrupt rule one might think we would consider the record of human government. We choose, instead, to continue to pin our hopes on the promises of negotiators who lack the ability to read their compasses.

Israel is the compass for international policy for good reason. David exposed that reason to Goliath just before he brought him down. "I'm going to take your head from you today, Goliath, so that all the world may know there is a God in Israel," the young warrior announced. His cry continues to haunt the nations today. Every nation has some godly people living inside its borders, but the system that rules each nation is led, to greater and lesser degrees, by the "prince of this world" and his worshipers.

Israel is different from other nations—not because the people living there comprehend truth. In point of fact, few of them presently understand their real situation. This does not nullify the fact, however, that what David said remains true—there is a God in Israel, and anyone who touches Israel has to contend with this God. That is why it is deadly to mishandle this volatile portion of supernatural real estate.

Touching another person's private property is serious business. Especially when that person is God. It has nothing to do with emotions and whether you prefer Jews or their Islamic neighbors; nor does it have to do with whether you want peace or war. It has to do with the original script and the power behind the Author to enforce His original intention.

From all appearances, Yitzhak Rabin was a peacemaker at heart. As a good soldier and general who poured his blood into Israel, he was under tremendous pressure to exchange land for peace. At his funeral the President of the United States passionately declared, "This man's dream did not die with the assassin's bullet, but so long as Israel pursues its present course of peace, the United States of America will continue its full support."

The carrion birds of other nations stood by and looked on the burial site, searching for whatever treasures might have been unearthed in the freshly dug grave of a fallen leader. Half faces peered from behind closed systems, seeking fresh opportunity, while the microphone minstrels declared with professional somber tones, "No one knows what Rabin's death will do to the peace process."

31

But someone does know what such events do to the peace process. Anyone who cares to know may read and find out. The answer was recorded for us hundreds of years ago.

> I will also gather all nations, And bring them down to the Valley of Jehoshaphat; And I will enter into judgment with them there On account of My people, My heritage Israel, Whom they have scattered among the nations; They have also divided up My land. (Joel 3:2, NKJV)

Every time men (either those from within Israel or elsewhere) go to the leadership of Israel and begin to pressure them to divide God's land, the world moves one step closer to Armageddon. Listen to God's clear warning to the Gentile nations:

> Proclaim this among the nations: Prepare for war! Wake up the mighty men, Let all the men of war draw near, Let them come up. Beat your plowshares into swords And your pruning hooks into spears; Let the weak say, 'I am strong.' ...Let the nations be wakened, and come up to the Valley of Jehoshaphat; For there I will sit to judge all the surrounding nations (Joel 3:9-10-12 NKJV).

Three Facts Need to Be Considered

(1) God has established His ownership of Israel by calling it "My land."

(2) He promises to judge the nations that scatter His people and part His land.

(3) He names the location for the final judgment (a battle) as the Valley of Jehoshaphat—Armageddon, in Israel.

Anytime men sit down to discuss "peace talks" that concern dividing Israel, they are using a contradiction in terms. God says such negotiations signal war. Ultimately they signal the "grand-daddy of all wars" in the lush Valley of Meggido, where Napoleon once fought. According to the Apostle John's birds-eye view of this day, demonic powers will eventually motivate various international leaders to unify and descend upon Israel. This will lead to a direct attack upon the Israeli policy of statehood, which will lead to international intervention in the form of war.

John describes this cataclysmic event, "...they are the spirits of devils, working miracles, which go forth unto the kings of the earth and of the whole world, to gather them to the battle of that great day of God Almighty. ...And he gathered them together unto a place called in Hebrew tongue Armageddon" (Revelation 16:14,16 emphasis added).

The Catalyst for War—Jerusalem

On July 30, 1980, the Israeli parliament (the Knesset) declared Jerusalem to be the eternal and indivisible capital of Israel. This stance will become the catalyst for Armageddon. The stubbornness of the Jews against giving up Jerusalem will lead to the war to end all wars. Israel will never agree to surrender the city of Jerusalem. God's plan, as revealed in the Scriptures, forbids it. Their ancient neighbors will never settle for anything less than Jerusalem. PLO Chairman Yasser Arafat made this clear at the outset of the "peace talks" when he said, "Jerusalem belongs to the Palestinians also." He is joined in this by an international chorus.

Shortly after Prime Minister Rabin's assassination in 1995, television programs were flooded with international opinions. One of the key subjects discussed was the so-called "fanatical notion" that the Jews have a divine right to the land of Israel. Abba Eban declared that such a possibility was "outside the realm of reality." James Baker and Margaret Fitzpatrick from the United States said as much—and passionately insisted that returning or giving away "acquired land" was the only alternative to peace. But such an ideology is short-sighted. It fails to deal with two vital questions.

When the demand comes to give up some or all of Jerusalem, should Israel comply? And how much land should Israel surrender in order to please the world?

As well meaning as they may be, statesmen who exclude any possibility of God will never be satisfied until Israel surrenders everything. God, on the other hand, will never be satisfied until Israel has everything He promised to Abraham and David. That is what Armageddon is all about.

3

Israel's Defender

In light of present realities, Israel needs a defender. Goliaths are still waiting to intimidate and conquer her. She is both a tired, old warrior and a feisty young trooper. She began in Abraham, yet she is having to begin again. She has risen from the dust, but the dust still sweeps over her borders.

Israel stays alive through war. Men say war can be avoided through negotiations. In a real sense, however, negotiations are a form of war. Through opposing ideologies, one man prevails and another surrenders.

"No blood is shed in negotiations," some will contend. But history disproves this thinking. Negotiations often lay the groundwork for major battles. Grandchildren often fight the battles their grandfathers negotiated. The Bible calls this process "making ungodly alliances."

"Blessed are the peacemakers," (Matthew 5:9) was never intended to drive men who have God's mandate to compromise God's intentions. This is what makes the Scriptures relevant with regard to Israel's dilemma over dividing her land.

Remember, "There *is* a God in Israel." He is a sovereign who has given a clearly defined mandate for the land and its people.

Certainly it is wise for any nation to negotiate whenever possible with regard to all negotiable items. Civil rights for all people within the framework of the law of the land stem from good negotiation. Hacking up the distinct identity and divine purpose of a nation for the sake of appeasing the few, however, is like selling the home place to buy toys for the children.

God set Israel's borders from ancient times. Men have removed those divinely driven stakes and have embarrassingly shrank her, but when the giants around her begin to attack what little portion she has, as they did in the 1967 Yom Kippur War, Israel fights and reclaims what is rightfully hers anyway.

For Israel to attempt to comfort herself in land give-a-ways for present peace is folly, for the results of such actions are bound to come back later in the form of blood. This is not to say that non-Jews should have no place in Israel. From the beginning, God commanded Israel to treat all its citizens with equity, but He never intended that Israel be anything but one undivided nation.

On the authority of the Scriptures, negotiating for peace by land give-a-ways is a battle won without blood, on the way to a war flowing with it—at Armageddon. Because Goliath has a big appetite—and many friends with whom he wishes to banquet—he will not be satisfied until David's sovereignty is annihilated.

Messiah's Temple

When David, as King of Israel, had sufficiently conquered all Israel's enemies during his reign, he had time to go into phase-two of God's mandate to build a house of worship in Israel. It would be the forerunner of Messiah's Temple during the millennial restoration (the 1,000 years following Jesus' return to earth).

David never got to build that house for God, as he desired. God sent Nathan the prophet to David with a word that adjusted the king's plans. Leaping thousands of years ahead in time, God revealed to David several unmistakable truths that are slated to take place during the millennial reign of Messiah Jesus at His second advent.

With a personal word of encouragement through Nathan, God reminded David that he was, after all, a shepherd lad whom He had made to be vice-regent over Israel. God would, therefore, build a house for David, rather than David building a house for God.

> Moreover I will appoint a place for My people Israel, and will plant them, that they may dwell in a place of their own and move no more; nor shall the sons of wickedness oppress them anymore, as previously. (2 Samuel 7:10, NKJV)

Israel, as a people, is guaranteed divine right to live in the land of Israel without threats and wars. The day is coming when Israel will no longer have to live with constant negotiations for its rights in the world community. With the throne of David restored, nations will come to them. But before this happens, Israel will have to pay a heavy price to maintain her rights. This is what God said to David:

> When your days are fulfilled and you rest with your fathers, I will set up your seed after you, *who will* come from *your body*, and I will establish his kingdom. He shall build a house for My name, and I

will establish the throne of his kingdom forever. I will be his Father, and he shall be My son. If he commits iniquity, I will chasten him with the rod of men and with the blows of the sons of men. (2 Samuel 7:12-14, NKJV)

This word from God has a double fulfillment. David's natural son, Solomon, did build a temple for God that was unequaled by anything in the civilized world. Even the temple guards had gold on their coats of mail. But it is evident by what Nathan says next that the temple to which God is referring is both a temporary and an eternal temple. "And your house and your kingdom shall be established forever before you. Your throne shall be established forever" (2 Samuel 7:16). Clearly this is referring to Jesus at His coming, assuming David's throne.

David himself conceded this by saying, "...thou hast spoken also of thy servant's house for a great while to come" (2 Samuel 7:18-19).

After a period of worship, David went on to position Israel again according to her divine calling, "And what one nation in the earth is like thy people, even like Israel, whom God went to redeem for a people to himself?..." (2 Samuel, 7:23).

Many Gentiles choke at this statement and run all over the history books attempting to explain the end of the age. But we can keep a clear eye on the closing pages of history if we will avoid overestimating both the role and power of the Gentile nations, leaving divine history in its proper Middle Eastern setting. Even when the famed world class leader (antichrist) comes on the scene, to possess Jerusalem and eliminate Israel's status as a nation, we can go back to David's words and rest assured that, "There *is* a God in Israel."

A Gentile Amen

As a Gentile, and now a Christian, I find great pleasure in God's eternal promise to David. I take deep satisfaction in God's sovereign choices. He has chosen Israel in a unique way from among the nations. Amen, so be it.

Let church triumphalism die, so that the saints from among all nations may rejoice in God's plans. Is it not enough that we Gentiles have been offered present salvation and future glory? Must we also demand that God forget His promises to those whom He first called and loved and made an eternal covenant with? After all, if God can renege on Israel, what's to keep Him from also reneging on the Church?

Israel's present sufferings are due in part to their spiritual blindness concerning their spiritual mandate. God said clearly that He called Israel to be a spiritual light to the nations. If career politicians and bloated historians can't allow for the possibility of God's will in Israel, surely the Church of Jesus Christ should stand in support of it. Sadly, such has rarely been the case. History shows the Church to be an ally of the infidel more often than of God's plan for His people and land.

The Church could be a great ally of Israel. And since the revival of the 1970's, there has been an increasing understanding in the Church of Israel's continuing role in God's scheme of things. The sound of Hebraic music is flourishing in the Church. Support from many Christian denominations is providing thousands of dollars for Israel annually. But we have a long way to go.

In our sermons, we refer to the Jews as those who rejected and crucified Jesus. Officially Israel did reject the Messiah. "He came unto his own, and his own received him not" (John 1:11).

But who made up the first church if not Jews? Who were the people in the Upper Room? Catholics, Protestants, Orthodox? On whom did the Holy Spirit fall if not Jews, who in turn preached to Jews. Acts 6:7 says, "And the word of God increased; and the number of the disciples multiplied in Jerusalem greatly; and a great company of the priests were obedient to the faith."

Like a young stallion resisting the saddle, Israel is paying the price for her rebellion. But Israel is not going to pay the price for the Church's indifference to her plight. If we truly love God and desire to give Him pleasure, let us at least weep for Israel as He must be doing. We know how He feels. Jesus said, "O Jerusalem, Jerusalem,... how often would I have gathered thy children together, even as a hen gathereth her chickens under her wings, and ye would not!" (Matthew 23:37).

In 1995, Paul and I wept when Yitzhak Rabin was assassiated. We wept that a heart filled with love for Israel had been stilled. We wept for the days ahead. But we went back to David's promise and we rejoiced that Israel has a Defender, One who will never abandon her, even though all nations eventually shall. He is the One who shall restore the Tabernacle of David and establish the borders of Israel forever.

4

Securing Israel's Borders

Israel was a beleaguered, disjointed nation when David came to the throne. A greedy, rebellious Saul had failed to lead Israel to victory. The Philistines had humiliated the royal house of Israel and impaled Saul's body on a pole, after totally defeating his army.

David subsequently came to the throne and for forty years he led Israel to its pinnacle of power. He united the twelve tribes and caused them to establish their nationhood. Superimposed over David was the kingdom of heaven, which he exuberantly acknowledged.

David would never have made Eban's statement that the Scriptures are "outside the bounds of reality." Just the opposite, David said, "For by thee I have run through a troop; and by my God have I leaped over a wall ...the word of the Lord is tried: he is a buckler [shield, defender] to all those that trust in him" (Psalms 18:29-30).

Israel is a monarchy. We all know that a king has not been in residence since 70 A.D., but this does not change this established fact. What we are looking at in Israel today is an interim government. If we understand this, we will know that no non-royal statesman inside Israel will ever settle the land questions that continually plague her. Interim rulers do not have the authority to change the borders set down by the King. Yet the pressures of commoners against an "absentee monarchy" make it difficult for the interim ruler to maintain the peace. It causes decent men to sacrifice land that is certain to be recalled. Sooner or later, the King will demand His property lines be restored. Israel's borders will be secured only when a descendant of David sits on the throne of Israel. Israel's government will one day return to a monarchy.

We know these things to be true by virtue of a question posed by the Jewish disciples of Jesus, "Wilt thou at this time restore again the kingdom to Israel?" (Acts 1:6).

"It is not for you to know the times or the seasons, which the Father hath put in His own power" (Acts 1:7), Jesus answered, just as succinctly as the question had been posed.

Here again we see what David declared to Goliath, "There is a God in Israel." He is the God who fathered creation, and He declared His Son to be the King (See Psalms 2). Only He can say when the kingdom in Israel will be re-established, but He has set a time and it will be restored by the King.

When Gabriel came from the presence of the Father to a Jewish maiden named Miriam (Mary), he identified the King as "...Jesus...the Son of the Highest; and the Lord God will give Him the throne of His father David" (Luke 1:31-32, NKJV). If this were not sufficient evidence, the next line spoken by Gabriel brings us once again to the subject of Israel's monarchy: "And He will reign over the

42

house of Jacob forever, and of His kingdom there will be no end" (Luke 1:33, NKJV).

Jesus opened His earthly ministry by saying, "Repent, for the kingdom of heaven is at hand" (Matthew 4:17). Is this to say that Israel's kingdom and the kingdom of heaven are one in the same? Not quite, but almost.

Israel, as originally intended, and Heaven have the same King. It may be better to say that among nations, Israel is the primary nation within the universal kingdom of heaven. Just as all other nations will have a local body politic during the Millennium, when Messiah comes again, Israel will be a nation under none other than their prince, David. Jeremiah said, "...they shall serve the Lord their God, And David their king, Whom I will raise up for them" (Jeremiah 30:9, NKJV). (See also Hosea 3:4-5.) This may challenge our overstuffed logic, but according to the Scriptures, David will be resurrected at the coming of Jesus and he will rule as the prince over his people, under King Jesus. Israel's borders will then reach from the Euphrates to the Nile.

The coming kingdom of heaven and the restoration of the kingdom to Israel is not a new doctrine spun by the Church within the past few years. It is not the emotional reaction of Zionists hoping to hold on to their property. Indeed, the first Jewish believers in Jerusalem knew and discussed the subject of Israel's restored monarchy at their first council meeting at Jerusalem, after Jesus' ascension.

The Jerusalem Council

Council debate was ensuing among the first Jewish believers about the salvation of the Gentiles by the Messiah. Paul and Barnabas had just finished relating the

43

miracles and wonders God was performing among the Gentiles, when James took the floor and began to remind them: "Simon has declared how God at the first visited the Gentiles to take out of them a people for His name. And with this the words of the prophets agree, just as it is written" (Acts 15:14-15, NKJV).

"After this I will return and will build again the tabernacle of David," James said. But what did he mean by the phrase, "After this?" He meant that, after the largely Gentile Church has come to God and completed its role in evangelizing Gentile nations, God will return to Israel and take up where He left off in 70 A.D. when Jerusalem fell. At this time He will re-establish David's kingdom in Israel.

"After This"

Human history is coming to the close of the period referred to in Acts as "after this." "After this I will return and will build again the Tabernacle of David." After this—the completion of the Church Age—Jesus will return and set about to restore the glory of Israel that David and Solomon enjoyed at the peak of their reigns. The restoration will begin with a change of heart, which is where true restoration in any nation or person begins. It will then spread until Israel becomes a natural attraction, as well as a spiritual beacon, to the whole earth.

Until that day, however, the Gentiles will continue to dominate the world scene. This means that all nations have an active part to play in the events of the last days. For this reason we shall now expand our focus to include the world community of nations. In the next chapter we are going to take a look at the spirit behind world powers.

5

The Spirit Behind World Powers

Remember ancient Rome? It's only been 1,900 years since the Romans showed the Church what the "home office" thinks of God's plans.

National leaders operate from a power base. Throughout history few of them have been based on God. In the next few pages, we are going to unravel a system with a plan that has been in the world for thousands of years. Beginning with great leaders of the past, we are going to uncover the age-old spirit behind world powers, and we are going follow it to its final conclusion.

For several years my husband, Paul, and I have traveled in what was called the Eastern Bloc. We have passed through all kinds of strict border crossings in almost every communist operation, including the Soviet Union. But nowhere in those countries were we warned more about strict controls than when we were preparing to go into East Germany. Towers manned by guards armed with machine guns sat ready to stop any would-be violator. While stony faces checked and rechecked credentials at the point of crossing, one could just sense the seriousness of their intentions.

We had the opportunity to be among the first to travel into East Germany once the communist system had crumbled in that nation and the Berlin Wall came tumbling down. But when we arrived at the border, we were unprepared for what we actually experienced. Empty towers standing as monuments of mockery signaled a power that had suddenly evaporated. Once-stern guards no longer peered into vehicles with a passionless search, but stood, instead, casually waving cars through as if they were a construction crew. The spiritual impact of that moment is what this message is all about.

"All the power of the old system is gone," I said to my family. "The power over East Germany has been broken. The evil prince that has ruled this nation from the heavenlies has—at least for the moment—been pulled down!" It was a tremendous experience to see the fresh corpse—the physical remains—of an evil spiritual power lying before our eyes.

Creation is not a toy. God made everything with a purpose. It gives God pleasure to see things fulfill the purpose for which they were designed.

If we could turn our cameras to the table of world government from which the sovereign God reigns, we would hear this declaration: "You are worthy, O Lord, To receive glory and honor and power; For You created all things, And by Your will they exist and were created" (Revelation 4:11, NKJV).

The glory, the honor, and the power of creation belong to God. When Satan deceived man into sinning, God not only lost intimate fellowship with humanity, He lost a relationship with all His creation on earth. Under sin, a curse was set in motion. Thorns grew up quickly beside the real plants, the nature of animals turned wild, and the glory, honor, and powers of the earth became servants to Satan. We know this is true by virtue of the death that presently pervades everything. We also have the verbal witness of the one behind the corruption.

Understanding Kingdoms

Immediately after the Son of God declared His divine mission on earth, the Bible says Satan visited Him with an offer:

> Again, the devil took Him [Jesus] up on an exceedingly high mountain, and showed Him all the kingdoms of the world and their glory. And he said to Him, "All these things I will give You if You will fall down and worship me." (Matthew 4:8-9, NKJV)

Satan is in charge of the kingdoms of the world, but to get hold of what this actually means we need to probe into the meaning of the word "kingdoms."

Growing up in a rural setting, I sometimes had an opportunity to watch people transact the buying and selling of land. When a person wanted to purchase a piece of property, both the buyer and the seller would go out and "walk" the land. They established borders and declared that a certain area belonged to said property.

The root of the word "kingdom" means *to pace with the foot*, to *walk off the boundaries of the property in question.*

And this is precisely what happened between Jesus and Satan during that period of time in the mountains that we call "the Temptation." Together, the Prince of Life and the prince of death walked through the kingdoms of this world. Imagine what they must have seen as they peered into the small realms of power in the cities, in the military garrisons, in the marble halls of government. Jesus and Satan visited them all.

Satan, a great prince whose vanity had corrupted his God-given power, had established certain realms on this earth as his power base. At the base of economics he had put *greed*. At the base of *fame* he had put *pride*. At the base of *fallen nature* he had put *selfishness*. And at the base of nations he had put *power hungers*.

Then Satan approached Jesus with his power base and tempted Him to change His allegiance. What Satan literally said to Jesus was this: "Money, fame, man's nature, and nations were once under your authority, but now they all belong to me. You can have them back if you will acknowledge me as sovereign over all. Instead of God, make me your sovereign and you can rule the earth just as you planned in the beginning."

In that moment Jesus stood face to face with the greed of buying power, the pride of "being somebody," the inherent drive to satisfy self at any cost, and the thrust of superior authority. It was an offer that translated into luxury, admiration, ease, and personal exaltation. But one single truth burning within His righteous nature came rising to the surface, "...Get thee hence, Satan: for it is written, Thou shalt worship the Lord thy God, and him only shalt thou serve" (Matthew 4:10).

The walk was over. Jesus had paced off all Satan's property and He didn't buy one square inch of his offer.

The Prince of the World System

Presently, Satan is still in charge of the systems of this world. This is not to say that every leader is corrupt, but it does expose the source of the world's power base, and Satan is still making his offer to lesser princes.

The price of Satan's property is death, and death separates. It separates the body from the soul. It separates each species of creation from the others. We live in a world of separation and disunity. The weather fights the earth through climatic hostility—droughts, storms, earthquakes. The earth fights its inhabitants through poor productivity and limited ability to handle excessive use. The inhabitants of the earth fight each other for survival and territorial advantages. World peace from within our own resources is a myth.

Who can go into the oceans and stop species of sea-life from devouring one another? Who will go to the deserts and stop the snake from eating the mouse who eats the spider who eats the insects? Who will go to the high Sierras, or the arid plains of Africa, and bring a truce between the lion and the zebra—or the wildebeest?

Man's *observation* of creation has led to the false assumption that *communication* among all families is possible. The people who are calling for *earth awareness* envision a harmonious world of natural reciprocity, but the truth is that *aggressive survival* is the motivating force behind nature in its cursed state.

In a remote Middle Eastern village, a giant bird flew down and picked up a small child and flew away with it. No doubt the bird's survival was at stake, and even if its form were painted in brilliant hues as a tribute to the beauty of nature, that would not prevent a hungry bird from committing a violent act.

49

The breakdown in nature is irreparable in the hands of man. Even if every human being alive agreed to lay down arms and hold hands, we would not bring in the Millennium.

There is a power base behind nature that must be dealt with before peace will reconcile all creation. Imagine fifty hungry lions turned loose on your congregation on the next worship day, and you will catch a glimpse of what Satan really wants to do with the followers of Jesus.

The Definition of "Anti"

Originally the prefix *anti* meant "*in place of.*" Later it also came to mean "against." There is a spirit in the world that keeps trying to take the place of Christ; it is against Him.

Christ, or Messiah, means the Anointed One. The Anointed One is the "Appointed One" whom God has chosen to head up the governments of this world.

Governments are spirit-led.

Isaiah tells us clearly that world government will one day be upon the shoulders of God's appointed leader. But for thousands of years Satan has hoped to put someone else "in place of" God's man. Thus, we have a strong spirit on the earth at work against Christ. The nearer His coming into power, the more fiercely this spirit works to prevent His coronation.

In the next chapter we are going to take a look at the profile of a man who is coming on the scene in the Middle East, a man who will personify the spirit of antichrist. Three famous forerunners tell us what we may expect from him.

6

War Is Coming!

War is coming. More war is on the horizon. The greatest war the earth has even seen is yet to be fought. God designated dozens of references and one entire book to its description. Daniel and Revelation are the most futuristic books on the market. They describe in great detail what the human race can expect in the closing days of this era.

One day soon, the embodiment of all Satan has ever dreamed will be set in motion. Moral sins were never Satan's ultimate plan. The thrill of immorality, greed, and temporary glory is only junk jewelry Satan has hung around the necks of spiritually blind people to keep them distracted from his real purpose.

Arthur Pink has said that, "The realm in which the archenemy works is not the moral but the spiritual. He calls into question the Word of God...." (Arthur Pink, *Gleanings from Genesis*, Chicago Illinois: Moody Press, 1950, p. 5.) For a handful of junk, the world is helping Satan to bring about an earth-wide attempt to overthrow God's rule on this planet. The heart of the battle will be the Middle East, but the heat of the battle will be worldwide.

Apostasy—divorce from God—is a worldwide problem. At this point in history no nation is left that is truly godly. Do we have godly people? Yes. Do we have God-led, God-honoring nations? No. This is the hour when every man is seeking his own things. Worldwide lawlessness is covering the earth like a foam. No nation is exempt. Political leaders have never suffered more contempt worldwide than they do today. People no longer care about the common good—it is every man for himself. Self-worshiping humanism is rampant.

The world is ripe for a leader who can promise it all—and deliver.

The Islamic Wave

Now let us return to our opening statement and see what all this has to do with the coming "Islamic wave." It is amazing how few students of prophecy pay any attention to this overwhelmingly large bloc of people—Muslims. This is amazing in light of the fact that the Islamic people are key players in end-time events.

Rome had a big footprint when Jesus was born. Once again the nations have turned their magnifying glass toward Rome, but history will not be decided in Rome. The Bible makes it blatantly clear that human history will close in the Middle East—specifically in Israel. This means that the peoples of the Middle East will be among the key players.

Tracing the regions of the eight ancient world empires on the map, you will also discover the Middle East to be the heart of the Islamic wave. There is a belt that stretches across the midriff of the earth from Northern Africa all the way to India that is purely Islamic, with the exception of one tiny state called Israel. It is this one state that is a constant source of irritation under the belt of the Islamic giant. And one day soon he is going to awaken and do everything within his power to eradicate this "infidel" intruder.

"But," you may question, "what about all the religious fervor we see among the Hindus? The Buddhists? The Baha'is? These religions are older than Christianity, with loyal followers for generations, and some of them are also creating waves—especially the spread of Buddhism from east to the west."

What about the ancient religions before Christ? Would it be fair to let Jesus tell us about them? Jesus said, "All who ever came before Me are thieves and robbers..." (John 10:8, NKJV). Ancient religious leaders and their philosophies are nothing more than misguided religionists who have robbed much of the human race of their part in the Kingdom of God.

God created man. The human race belongs to God, but Satan has sent religious thieves into the world to deceive God's flock—and destroy their souls in hell. We know this is true because Jesus said, "The thief does not come except to steal, and to kill, and to destroy. I have come that they may have life, and that they may have it more abundantly" (John 10:10, NKJV).

Ancient religious leaders before Christ are thieves. But what about the one coming after Him that is so powerful he is identified in the Scriptures as antichrist—the very antithesis of Christ—the one who will seek to take the very seat of international government *in place of Christ*?

Do you recall the words of Isaiah when he prophesied of the coming Messiah that "The government will be upon

His shoulder....Of the increase of His government and peace there will be no end" (Isaiah 9:6-7, NKJV). Even forever?"

There is coming a religio-political *movement* headed up by Satan's strongest "territorial strong man" that will sweep the midsection of this earth, from North Africa all the way to Russia and east to India, with staggering swiftness.

This antichrist political storm will become *incarnate* (become flesh) in the form of a world-class political leader unlike any person we have ever known. He will have a religious support base more powerful than any empire the world has ever seen. It will be what John called the "false prophet" and will include what is now called by secular political analysts the "Islamic Belt." No politician who does not have the approval of the Islamic people is going to make great headway in the Middle East. True, the antichrist is going to sign a treaty with Israel, but this man will have drafted that treaty in harmony with the Islamic agenda as well. In conjunction with this Islamic backing of antichrist's policy, will be the apostate church in the West. Because true, biblical faith is being rejected in favor of a pantheistic philosophy that sees man and creation as gods, the West will flow with the policy which satisfies its own economic interests.

We do well to remember that, until Christopher Columbus discovered the Americas in 1492, the Islamic world controlled all trade between the East and West. The treasures and technology of China could only be had in the West after they had passed through Constantinople (Istanbul, Turkey)—the capital of the eastern Roman Empire that was totally engulfed by Muhammad. Muslim control of goods and their financial gain through "handling charges" became a burden the West wanted to circumvent. This sent Columbus west, looking to avoid the Islamic belt of the Middle Ages. Again, in the end days, there will be a restructuring and tightening of the old Islamic financial stronghold. Could it be the numbering system 666? Certainly Islam is a power base to be reckoned with.

Listen to the words of various political experts as they talk about the events the prophets so carefully recorded thousands of years ago.

Gilles Kepel, a French expert on Islam, said: "To a certain extent, Islamic forces have already won. What we're seeing is the re-Islamization of the entire region, the alteration of basic patterns of life." And he adds, "Europe is not immune!"

According to an international cross section of Middle East, Arab, and western scholars, the ideologies of the secular and nationalistic Arabs have been "eclipsed" by the fall of the Soviet Union, and the inability of the Arab states to take a position in the Gulf War. This Islamic world, as a result, is rapidly being filled with *Islamic fervor.*

Judith Miller, author of *The Islamic Wave*, declares, "There is a yearning for the lost greatness of the Islamic civilization of the 9th and 10th centuries. Whereby the new slogan has become 'Islam is the solution!'"

Hassan Al Turabi, chief of the Islamic Front in Sudan, who earned his doctorate at the Sorbonne, helped to write that country's Islamic laws, which includes the death penalty for *apostasy.* Turabi says,

> Islam is becoming temporal [timely, secular]. You in the West had better get used to it, and you should not be afraid of it. We are not your enemy. Besides, objectively, the future is ours.

Who could argue with this conclusion when you remember that in 1995 a Muslim called one million Americans to the nation's capital in Washington, D.C. to declare a celebration of unity. It was a gathering that received extensive nation-wide television coverage.

According to the Prophet Daniel, the antichrist will rule the Islamic Belt region of the ancient Roman Empire. His rise, like that of Alexander the Great, will be fast and far-reaching, and then, as Alexander, he will fall overnight.

Daniel also seems to say that the antichrist will come out of the area of the Roman Empire that covered the ancient Grecian Empire.

> And as I was considering, behold, an he goat came from the west on the face of the whole earth *[synecdoche*—meaning the civilized world]...and the goat [Greece] had a notable horn between his eyes. And he came to the ram that had two horns [Medo-Persia]...and smote the ram, and brake his two horns.... Therefore the he goat [Greece] waxed very great: and when he was strong, the great horn was broken [Alexander the Great died]; and for it came up four notable ones [the Grecian Empire divided into four powers: Greece, Turkey, Syria, and Egypt]....(Daniel 8:5-8)

> And out of one of them came forth a little horn, which waxed exceeding great...toward the pleasant land. And it waxed great even to the host of heaven....Yea, he magnified himself even to the prince of the host, and by him the daily sacrifice was taken away...." (Daniel 8:9-11)

As you continue reading this chapter of Daniel, it becomes quite clear that this man (the little horn from one of the four divisions of the Grecian Empire which was within the old Roman Empire) is the antichrist who will come on the scene in the last days and seek to establish himself in Jerusalem as "savior" of a world in crisis.

This does not say that the antichrist lives in one of the four ancient divisions of the Grecian Empire. He could have ancestral roots in one of these divisions, yet live in Europe, as some scholars believe. In any event, he will be a man of such skill he will impress a foolish world by his sheer arrogance against God and the people of God.

> He shall speak pompous words against the Most High, and shall *persecute the saints* of the Most High, and shall intend to change times and law. Then the saints shall be given into his hand for a time and times and half a time [three and one-half years]. But the court shall be seated, and they shall take away his dominion, to consume and destroy it forever. Then the kingdom and dominion, and the greatness of the kingdoms under the whole heaven, shall be given to the people, the saints of the Most High. His kingdom is an everlasting kingdom, and all dominions shall serve and obey Him. This is the end of the account....(Daniel 7:25-28, NKJV)

A pompous beginning for the antichrist, but what an ending! What a wave of power struggles is going to grip the politics of the Euro-Mediterranean and Middle East! There is coming a religio-political empowered wave of warfare in the Middle East that will shake the nations of the world as they have never been shaken. Oil embargoes, struggles over water rights, dislocated people, erratic weather patterns, plagues, missile exchanges, runaway inflation, and sporadic wars will continue to wash upon the troubled shores of all nations until the world cries out for a deliverer. The region of the old Roman Empire will then supply the cradle for the antichrist to appear. At the peak of antichrist's ruthless, unholy reign of power, the Son of God will come in a tidal wave of glory that will hit the buckle of the Islamic Belt and break its power so thoroughly that millions of men, women, and children will be set free in a day.

Wars are fought for months or years—but peace is always declared in a day. God has a wave of righteous government coming upon this earth that will totally subdue all opposition. And the result will be the salvation of millions—beginning with the Jews, spreading quickly among the Muslims then over the face of the whole earth.

> Therefore say to the house of Israel, Thus says the Lord God; 'I do not do this for your sake, O house of Israel, but for mine holy name's sake, which ye have profaned among the heathen, whither ye went. And I will sanctify my great name, which was profaned among the heathen, which ye have profaned in the midst of them; and the heathen shall know that I am the Lord, saith the Lord God, when I shall be sanctified in you before their eyes. (Ezekiel 36:22-23)

The Islamic religion has been rising and falling for the past 1,200 years. It could never carry out its full intent because the time had not been right. Its greatest performance will be its last performance. Yet out of Islam's grave error in worship, God is going to bring Israel to its knees in every respect. Politically, they will be devastated; militarily, they will be fighting for their life. But above and beyond their physical state, the heart of Israel is going to humble itself and turn to God in full surrender. As a result of Israel's revival, they will pick up their divine and ancient mandate, and then they will go out and bring the knowledge of God to all the nations.

The Islamic wave is coming. It will be furious and short-lived, because it is destined to be washed away by the glorious wave of God! Before this wave goes out to sea forever, God is going to call all nations to give account for their choice of power.

7

Two Great Waves of Power

There are two great waves of power coming on the earth. But before we look at them, let us briefly review the history of the two key players of the Middle East.

Ishmael Versus Isaac

Approximately 4,000 years ago, God was about to set in motion His predestined plan for saving the human race. He began by choosing a man named Abraham. Through him, God would establish the Messianic race that would give birth to God's Son on earth. The Messiah, in turn, would regain the earth for God through His sacrificial blood and His subsequent millennial restoration.

May I suggest that at this point Satan, knowing God's plan for Abraham, quickly set in motion his own plan for a world ruler. Through Abraham, Satan would produce a "false messiah" who would carry out his plans and cause all nations to worship him instead of God.

The two great "supernatural plans of the ages" unfold in the life of Abraham in this manner: God appeared to Abraham when he was ninety-nine years old, saying:

> ...Sarah your wife shall bear you a son, and you shall call his name Isaac; and I will establish My covenant with him for an everlasting covenant for his descendants after him. (Genesis 17:19, NASB)

One year later, Sarah, ninety years of age, bore a son to Abraham and they named him Isaac.

- Abraham fathered Isaac.
- Isaac fathered Jacob [name changed to Israel].
- Israel fathered twelve sons.
- The twelve sons became the twelve tribes of Israel.
- One of these twelve tribes produced Jesus.

Jesus was the human form of God the Son, and heir to the world's throne—the same universal throne which Satan has desired to occupy since iniquity entered into him. I believe, in fact, it may have been Satan's jealousy of God's Son that prompted his rebellion in heaven many centuries ago. Satan desired to rule the world; but God chose His Son to rule instead. The Son accepted that awesome position, knowing that one day he would have to go into Satan's territory and fight him legally for the title to our planet.

Jesus accomplished universal control, including planet earth, by allowing himself to be killed and shed His innocent blood for the sins of man. While His physical body lay dead, He went into Satan's headquarters and confronted him in a legal battle. Jesus took the title to earth away from Satan in this battle and legally delivered the earth back to God.

That is the sum total of the plan of God initiated in Abraham and Sarah when He gave them Isaac.

However, just prior to the initiation of God's plan through the birth of Isaac, Satan set in motion his own scheme for establishing an earth-wide ruler who would deliver all nations to himself for worship. And just as God had done, Satan chose Abraham to give birth to his plot. Satan has always been the great counterfeiter.

Only sixteen years before Isaac was born to Abraham, Satan put despair into the mind of Sarah, "You are already past bearing age, Sarah," he whispered. "You should not deny poor Abraham an heir...go ahead, use your attractive young servant Hagar. Let her be a surrogate mother for you."

Read it in Genesis 16:1-2:

> Now Sarai Abram's wife bare him no children: and she had an handmaid, an Egyptian, whose name was Hagar. And Sarai said unto Abram, Behold now, the Lord hath restrained me from bearing; I pray thee, go in unto my maid: it may be that I may obtain children by her. And Abraham hearkened to the voice of Sarai.

Only sixteen more years to wait, Sarah! But through your doubt and despair Satan was able to set in motion a people that have laid claim to Messiah's city and land, and they will lend great assistance to the coming world dictator called the antichrist. Out of obedience to Sarah, Hagar the Egyptian bore a son to Abraham and named him Ishmael. Through impatience, Satan succeeded in bringing to birth a child who would carry out his plan to harass the Messianic race down through the centuries, all the way through the seven last years of human government and into the Battle of Armageddon.

When Ishmael—Satan's plan for a world ruler—was sixteen years old, Isaac—God's plan for a world ruler— was born. "For Sarah conceived and bore Abraham a son in his old age, at the set time of which God had spoken to him" (Genesis 21:2, NKJV).

The great supernatural war of the Middle East began at that precise moment. In time, Ishmael, the older son of Abraham, began to mock Isaac. It was a supernatural hatred that has been passed from generation to generation. Ishmael and his descendants, who form the Arab nations, have always despised Isaac and his descendants, who form the Jewish people.

When Satan tricked Abraham into fathering Ishmael, he was able to set in motion a nation of people who would despise the Messianic nation for as long as human government lasts. The Messianic nation has an unbroken history of harassment and threatened expulsion from the land of Israel by Ishmael's descendants. It is a spiritual grudge passed down by Ishmael, because, in fact, he was the one who got expelled from the land after he began to harass Isaac.

> Cast out this bondwoman and her son: for the son of this bondwoman shall not be heir with my son, even with Isaac. (Genesis 21:10).

Thus, Ishmael and Hagar were sent away. This was in partial fulfillment of the word God had personally spoken to Hagar when she was still pregnant, saying of Ishmael that he would be, "...a wild man [a champion of the desert]; his hand will be against every man, and every man's hand against him..." (Genesis 16:12).

Yet, in spite of His gruesome prediction, God also promised to bless Ishmael and his descendants, and He has. Today the Arabic people are among the greatest in number, wealth, and political power. In addition to their prosperity, they also have every right to God's new covenant of eternal life through faith in Jesus. Through the death and Resurrection of Jesus, all descendants of Ishmael have the same spiritual opportunities as any Gentile nation. There is evidence that an increasing number of them are beginning to wake up to this possibility. Traditionally, however, few have accepted God's offer of life in Jesus, because of a spiritual blindness which engulfed them approximately 1,500 years ago.

Islam

In the sixth century A.D., a mystical prophet named Muhammad burst upon the Middle East with fanatical determination to convert the world to the worship of Allah. Through frequent murders of resistant heathen and intense hatred for Jews and Christians, the Islamic faithful began to increase rapidly in number. Throughout history they maintained their fervor based on three basic resolutions: (1) worldwide conversion to Islam; (2) expulsion of the Jews from the land of Israel; (3) control of the holy temple site, the very spot from which Jesus will one day rule the earth, according to the Bible.

The Temple site where Abraham offered Isaac, where David offered sacrifices, where Solomon worshiped Yahweh—God—is the one sacred spot Satan envies most. Because it has been promised to Jesus, David's descendant, as the location of His throne and temple, Satan has put fanatical determination into the one billion followers of Muhammad to retain the Temple site for Allah. Today the Golden Dome of the Rock is the second most holy place in the Islamic world. Only Mecca, where Mohammed is buried, is considered greater.

In thinking of the nationality of the antichrist we are inclined to assume he must only satisfy Israel with his peace treaty. But since the peace treaty is based on war between Jews and Muslims, we should realize that the antichrist will also have the ability to satisfy the Islamic nations surrounding Israel.

With this brief history of Islam in mind, let's now look at the coming waves of power.

The May 1992 issue of *The New York Times* had a front cover photo that looked like white sea shells spread among the busy traffic lanes of a major city. Upon closer examination, I noticed it was a photograph that showed Muslims bowing at Friday prayers. The caption below the scene read, "The Islamic Wave."

In the Scriptures, a symbolic term for *people* is *"sea."* The apostle John records of the last generation of human government that he "...saw a beast rise up out of the sea..." (Revelation 13:1). That is, he saw a regional political move coming out of the people. John referred to this movement of the end days as the "great whore that sitteth upon many waters" (Revelation 17:1). This image suggests a great   unified political move of many peoples. The use of the word "whore" also tells us that this political move will be spirit-empowered, with religious goals with a united political agenda. The term "whore" in the Scriptures is used to denote spiritual corruption.)

Daniel's Four Empires

Approximately 600 years before John's Revelation, Daniel said he saw, "The four winds [spiritual powers] of the heaven strove upon the great sea [people].

And four great beasts [four world empires] came up from the sea [people] . . ." (Daniel 7:2).

In modern language, what Daniel saw was four spiritual powers moving in the heavens. Out of the various moves came four world empires among the people. Political power comes from the heavenly regions of either Satan, in the second heavens of space, or God, in the highest heavens.

The Scriptures recognize eight world empires: Egypt, Assyria, Babylon, Medo-Persia, Greece, Rome, revised Rome and the antichrist empire. History makes it clear that not one of these has been or will be empowered by God.

Other empires have come on the scene throughout the history of the human race. China was a progressive dynasty when the West was still an embryo. Great Britain influenced the whole world with Christianity and the English language. America has been a brief, but powerful economic phenomenon. But according to God's dictionary, only eight empires have formed the cast for His drama, four of which were given specific recognition:

1. Babylon
2. Medo-Persia
3. Greece
4. Rome

What Daniel saw in his vision was Babylon, Medo-Persia, Greece, and the Roman Empire at two different periods—Rome at the birth of Christ and Rome at the Second Coming of Christ. We might also note here that the empires that have formed and shaped the destiny of mankind according to the Scriptures are located around the Mediterranean Sea—and all have a history of badgering and persecuting Israel, the Messianic people, and the residence of Messiah's future temple on earth.

As tempting as it may be to recast the key players of the geopolitical end-times, the Bible has made it quite clear who will be fighting for world domination and why. But when I use the term "world domination," I do not mean to suggest that one person will seek to rule every nation on the face of the earth.

Quite often in the Scriptures, a synecdoche is used when speaking of wholes and parts. A synecdoche is when you use a whole to mean a part or vice-versa. For example, when the Bible says, "All the world went to be taxed," it means all the Roman world—not every person on the face of the earth.

The coming antichrist will not seek to rule the whole earth. Rather he will seek to control that region he sees as his world, and he will have the cooperation of the United Nations in doing so. From the Scriptures, the "world" the antichrist seeks to dominate will be the Middle East—and especially the land of Israel. But in order for him to achieve his goal, he will need an international political climate conducive to one man ruling a vast portion of land across the belly of the earth, as well as a large portion of the earth's population. I am referring to the Islamic world that stretches all the way from North Africa to India.

The coming "wave of Islam" predicted by the *New York Times* is tomorrow's headlines in advance. It makes complete sense once you see it in context of the visions of Daniel, as he describes the empires that have and will propel history to its final conclusion.

Daniel's Vision of the Beast

The word "beast," when it is used in the Scriptures in the context of end-time things, means "nations." When Revelation speaks of the antichrist as a "beast," it is telling us that it is an empire headed by a powerful leader. Daniel records that he saw four beasts—four world empires: Babylon (a lion), Medo-Persia (a bear), Greece (a leopard), Rome (a nondescript beast). (See Daniel 7:4-7.) These four empires came and went. But Daniel says of the nondescript beast—the Roman Empire—that it had ten horns. "I considered the horns, and behold, there came up among them another little horn, before whom there were three of the first horns plucked up by the roots: and behold, in this horn were eyes like the eyes of a man, and a mouth speaking great things" (Daniel 7:8). This describes the "antichrist empire" that will arise in the last days.

As Gentile rule is drawing to a close, the old Roman Empire will come back to life, politically speaking. One of its nations or political regions, headed by a man called in the Scriptures the "little horn," will overthrow three of its ten power bases and cast them out of the revived confederacy. This "little horn" is the political wizard, the antichrist. Of him, Daniel writes:

> And out of one of them came a little horn which grew exceedingly great toward the south, toward the east, and toward the Glorious Land [Israel]. And it grew up to the host of heaven; and it cast down some of the host and some of the stars to the ground, and trampled them. He even exalted himself as high as the Prince of the host; and by him the daily sacrifices were taken away, and the place of His sanctuary was cast down. Because of transgression, an army was

given over to the horn to oppose the daily sacrifices; and he cast truth down to the ground. He did all this and prospered. (Daniel 8:9-12, NKJV)

The Old Roman Empire

We need to stop here for a look back at the boundaries of the old Roman Empire. Today's idea of Rome is largely Europe. Many fine scholars see only Europe's role in the end-time events described by the prophets. Because of the economic and political power bases of the West, we have almost forgotten that Isaac's battle has always been with Ishmael—not with a European.

This is not to say that Europe will have no role in end-time events. The continent is one leg of the ancient Roman Empire, and it certainly has a role.

In the Book of Daniel, the king of Babylon had a dream where he saw the four key empires of divine history: Babylon, Medo-Persia, Greece, and Rome. In his dream the king saw Rome as the two legs of a man. When the Roman Empire came on the world scene it did, in fact, divide into two regions with two capitals. One capital was at Rome and ruled over a limited portion of Europe. The other capital was at Constantinople and ruled over the Middle East. Rome eventually became politically Christian, and Constantinople became politically Islamic. These two regions set the stage for the events that concern us in these closing days of history.

"Because of transgression," Daniel said, because of apostate Christianity in the West and Israel's blindness to its spiritual mandate to the nations, God is going to allow the cruel foot of ancient Rome to rise up once again and trample the civilized world for a brief period. Rome in Europe and Rome in the Middle East will cooperate to produce a godless, religious-backed political giant who will seek to overthrow God's eternal plan for Israel and the nations.

From these verses it is obvious that the antichrist empire's main thrust will be against the nation of Israel. Israel is the only nation of the end days that would possibly be practicing the "daily sacrifice" (offerings and animal sacrifices) in the Temple of God. And it is in Israel where Messiah will establish His government.

As for how long the antichrist's attack on Israel will be in force, the next verses reveal: "How long will the vision be concerning the daily sacrifices?...For two thousand three hundred days; then the sanctuary shall be cleansed" (Daniel 8:13-14 NKJV).

It is my understanding of the Scriptures that the nondescript beast—the Roman Empire—is the culmination of all ungodly empires. It embodies all the features, plans, and programs of all ungodly nations— past, present, and future. This is why Rome never officially died. Rome is the last embodiment of the spirit of Babylon, the spirit associated with the place where spiritual and political rebellion was birthed.

Since the day when Abraham turned his back on Babylon, the spirit of Babylon has plagued Abraham's natural descendants, as well as his descendant Jesus and His "seed," the Church. Babylonian-Romanism has been the womb of all self-worship, greed, immorality, and corrupt political powers that have dominated the western world since Constantine legalized Christianity in 313 A.D. For the past 1,700 years, the spirit of Rome [not the Catholic Church] has continually corrupted the Church and plagued true faith.

It is important to remember that empires are never purely political or religious. They are a combination of both.

Revised Rome and the antichrist empire (which comes out of it) are a combination of all ancient empires. This is made clear in the following two Scriptures. "Then the iron, the clay, the bronze, the silver, and the gold were crushed together [this is the image Nebuchadnezzar saw of the four world empires: Babylon, Medo-Persia, Greece, and Rome], and became like chaff from the summer threshing floors; the wind carried them away so that no trace of them was found. And the stone that struck the image became a great mountain and filled the whole earth" (Daniel 2:35, NKJV). A second verse is, "Now the beast which I saw was like a leopard, his feet were like the feet of a bear, and his mouth like the mouth of a lion. The dragon gave him his power, his throne, and great authority" (Revelation 13:2, NKJV).

Leopard, bear, lion—*Greece, Medo-Persia, Babylon.* The spirits of these three ancient, pagan kingdoms are all embodied in the one "spirit of Rome." Is it not possible that these three religio-political empires are the three unclean spirits that will come out of the mouth of the dragon and draw the nations to Armageddon?

John wrote, "And I saw three unclean spirits like frogs coming out of the mouth of the dragon, out of the mouth of the beast, and out of the mouth of the false prophet. For they are spirits of demons, performing signs, which go out to the kings of the earth and the whole world, to gather them to the battle of that great day of God Almighty" (Revelation 16:13-14, NKJV).

If we read on for a few verses—we see that the antichrist spirit is:

The great whore that sitteth upon many waters [people from all the eight great empire regions of Europe, the Mediterranean and Middle East]...With whom the kings of the earth have committed fornication, and the inhabitants of the earth have been made drunk with the wine of her fornication. (Revevelation 17:1-2)

8

The Profile of the Antichrist

When an individual who was not well-known, such as Saddam Hussein of Iraq in 1990, seeks status and power in a small, obscure country, and has every nation of the world on alert, the possibility that a leader identified in the Scriptures as the "antichrist" seems completely plausible.

Basically the "spirit of antichrist" is an attitude that says "we can save the world without Christ." A professor friend of ours once said to my husband and me after hearing of our encounter with Jesus, "It sounds nice, but education is the answer to the world's problems." Some media moguls feel certain that "celluloid master minds" will come riding in on a white horse with the solution. Financial elitists are confident of their monetary remedies. But it all boils down to one attitude: the spirit of antichrist is any plan that takes the place of God's remedy.

From time to time, however, a single individual stands up and says, "I not only have the solution, I am the Savior!" And then he sets out to create his own world by reshaping the present one. These men then become profiles of the person who will come to be known as the antichrist.

Caligula Caesar

In 37 A.D., Caligula Gaius Caesar came to the throne. His early life in military camps had earned him the nickname Caligula ("little boot")—because of the military shoes he wore.

He seems innocent enough. Doesn't he?

The Roman Emperor Tiberius was a great uncle to Caligula. When Caligula was preferred to Tiberius's grandson, Gemullus, to be emperor, Caligula adopted Gemellus as his own son. Now "Little Boot" not only seems innocent, he appears to be a man of compassion.

Indeed, history records that Caligula ruled with mercy and generosity during the first six months of his reign. But then the spirit of antichrist entered into him. He began to squander his wealth on entertainment and building projects. He banished or murdered most of his relatives, including Gemellus. One of Caligula's favorite pastimes was having people tortured and killed while he lounged around a sumptuous Roman feast. He even made his horse a consul. Finally Caligula declared himself a god and had temples built where sacrifices were offered to his honor. He even planned an image of himself to be worshiped in Jerusalem. In his own mind, he became Christ for the people. But in 41 A.D. Caligula was assassinated by his guards—to make way for another "human savior," Nero.

Nero

Eight years after Caligula, in 49 A.D., the Emperor Claudius married his niece Agrippina who had a young son, Nero. After the death of Claudius, Nero was declared emperor. During the first five years of Nero's reign, he exhibited both ability and generosity. He was noted for his willingness to be merciful and fair, and his rule was one of moderation, with the exception that, when he first came to power, he had Claudius's son poisoned.

After five years, however, Nero released the full portrait of the antichrist spirit. To please his mistress, he had his mother murdered. In order to marry his mistress, he had his young wife Octavia put to death. In a rage, a short time later, he kicked his mistress-wife Poppaea and killed her. He then had Claudius's daughter put to death for refusing to marry him, and he married someone else after having her husband killed. In addition to all his domestic blood-letting, Nero had his life-long friend, and tutor, Seneca, and his son killed, along with many notable Romans. But on a much larger scale, after Rome burned, in order to divert the blame from himself, Nero placed the blame on the Christians.

This set the stage for massive persecution of the church at Rome. Christians were burned at the stake, crucified, beheaded, fed to lions, sewed up in animal skins, and thrown to hungry dogs and mangled to death. They were tortured and pressured to renounce Christ and worship the Roman gods, not the least of whom was the emperor. But the Roman Senate declared Nero a tyrant only eleven short years after he ascended the throne, whereupon he committed suicide.

Adolph Hitler

Bringing our discussion into more modern times, we have one of the clearest portraits of the spirit of antichrist ever painted. Through the rise and fall of Adolph Hitler, we find the ancient pattern modernized and carried out with planes, tanks, and guns, as opposed to swords, horses, and crosses. However, the pattern actually varies very little.

Hitler was a struggling young artist who was brought up in the Catholic tradition. For several years he supported himself in Vienna, by painting, selling postcards, and hanging wallpaper. Certainly no one would have imagined that the young man hanging paper on their kitchen walls would one day be the cause of fifty million deaths!

At the outbreak of World War I, Hitler enlisted and was twice decorated for bravery. At the end of this war he gradually began to develop an ideology of German dominance in Europe. After attempting to seize control of the Bavarian government, Hitler was sentenced to nine months in jail. During this period he wrote the work *Mein Kampf* (*My Struggle*), in which he set forth his program for the restoration of Germany.

Certainly nothing seems too disturbing about his life so far. A little radical and racially prejudiced, he is just a young artist, a brave soldier, an idealistic patriot. What harm could he possibly do?

All human beings are created more or less equal in that one may have three talents, another one, another five, but life pretty well balances out our skills. One mortal can actually do very little in this world—unless he is supernaturally empowered.

One man sold out to God can convert millions on every continent. John Wesley and Billy Graham have proved that. One man sold out to Satan can kill millions on every continent—Hitler proved that.

On January 30, 1933, Hitler was appointed Chancellor of Germany, and the clearest portrait of the personification of antichrist the world has seen to date was begun. Suppressing all opposition and political protocol, and condensing a whole philosophy into the appealing phrase, "The Third Reich," the third great German Empire was born.

One year later, a number of sound-thinking German officials sensed the danger of Hitler's policies and publicly criticized him. These same men were promptly executed in the so-called "blood purge," and the portrait of antichrist began to emerge. Among those executed was one of Hitler's closest associates, thus making it quite evident that Hitler had no personal loyalty to friends. He also had no regard for treaties with nations. His obsession to remake the world took precedence over everything and everyone else.

Within eleven brief years, with a world in devastation and their own people hungry, a group of disillusioned German army officers attempted to assassinate this modern madman who called himself the "Fuehrer." When their attempt failed, unfortunately a movement known as "operation thunderstorm" had thousands of them rounded up and brutally put to death.

In piecing together various accounts of the war years, several traits become prominent in the behavior of Adolph Hitler and his worldwide portrayal of the coming antichrist:

- His self-delusion was rampant.
- He was convinced of his own infallibility.
- He had one loyalty—his own cause.
- He was obsessed with presumed enemies—his accusations bordered on paranoia.
- He was eventually without mercy.

Hitler was not a man of war but a master of crime. Through deliberate campaigns of extermination against Poles, Russians, and especially Jews, multiplied millions of unarmed people were murdered.

In the end he took the path of Nero and committed suicide.

Antichrist

With these three biographical sketches in mind, let us now take a look at the profile of the coming antichrist defined in the Scriptures. John wrote, "Little children, it is the last time: and as ye have heard that antichrist shall come, even now are there many antichrists; whereby we know that it is the last time" (1 John 2:18). "And every spirit that does not confess that Jesus Christ is come in the flesh is not of God..." (1 John 4:3, NKJV).

Both the attitude and spirit of antichrist are already in the world. In this century as in no other, they have worked to prepare the people for a massive deception. Remember, "anti" means "in place of." Many false prophets and religious leaders as well as political dictators have come in our lifetime to save the world without Christ. But the antichrist will be a master who will put all others to shame. He will envision himself as the world's answer.

To begin with, the antichrist will be a national leader with international clout. He, as did the three examples we just studied, will put himself above the law. The present and popular attitude of lawlessness, which has thrown a devilish cape across the face of the earth in the past forty years, is in preparation of the antichrist's appearance on the world scene.

Selfish "meism" psychology, humanistic body worship, nature worship, and atheistic mind worship have locked arms to cast God out of heaven and exalt man's throne on high. "Let no man deceive you by any means: for that day shall not come, except there come a falling away first...," Paul warns us (2 Thessalonians 2:3). The term translated as "falling away" means to divorce oneself. Today's people have not only entered into unprecedented divorce of each other, they have divorced themselves from God. We are a generation who will not be dictated to by anyone outside ourselves.

> For that day shall not come, except there come a falling away first, and that man of sin be revealed, the son of perdition; Who opposeth and exalteth himself above all that is called God, or that is worshipped; so that he as God sitteth in the temple of God, shewing himself that he is God" (2 Thessalonians 2: 3-4).

What a loaded statement Paul is making here in his description of the antichrist. For "that day," the "day of the Lord," the time the prophets have foretold when God will judge sin and set up His kingdom on earth, "that day" will not come until the earth becomes rebellious, irreligious, immoral, and self-serving. Then that "man of sin"—the kind of man who would appeal to a lawless generation—will be revealed.

The antichrist will be the kind of charming personality that will be rushed to the front cover of *Time* Magazine and called the man of the century. Television interviews will be numerous. A New York public relations firm will be employed to dress and groom him for a flawless performance. This man will become so intoxicated with his sudden rise to international prominence that he, as Hitler, will lose all sense of reason, and he will turn as Nero turned on the "religious people," and going into the house of worship in Jerusalem, the antichrist will declare himself to be God. This act should give us a clear picture of where the heart of the last great conflict will take place. The location will be Israel. It should also tell us that the antichrist will be a man in the region of Middle Eastern affairs.

81

Daniel 8 tells us the history of Greece under Alexander the Great. He relates the break-up of the Grecian Empire into four kingdoms: Greece, Turkey, Syria, Egypt. Then Daniel writes: "And in the latter time of their [the Grecian Empire] kingdom, when the transgressors are come to the full, a king of fierce countenance, and understanding dark sentences, shall stand up." This is clearly the antichrist, who is supernaturally empowered for the last seven years of human government. Although it is commonly held that the antichrist will come from northern Europe, this and numerous other Scriptures suggest that we need to take another look at this subject.

Micah called the antichrist, "the Assyrian" (Micah 5:5). Antichrist might well come from the territory Assyria ruled in ancient times, which also covers a portion of the Greek and Roman Empires. For this reason he is called the Syrian (Daniel 11:35-45); the Roman prince that shall come (Daniel 9:26-27); and the Grecian (Zechariah 9:13). In this author's judgment, it is quite possible that the antichrist could come from the general territory of the Middle East-Mediterranean region, at least by ancestral roots as stated earlier. This does not necessarily mean he would be of Middle Eastern nationality, however.

Tracing the ancestral inhabitants of Europe in order to pinpoint the nationality of the antichrist has been the number- one tool of eschatologists (those who study the end-times) for the past seventy-five years. Who is settled in what region—who was there initially—seems paramount. Yet, as I have read the various theories in relation to the Scriptures, I am not convinced that the nationality of the people in Europe is the key to discerning the origin of the antichrist. What may be more important than trying to trace specific nationalities is tracing the "divine movement" of the Holy Spirit in specific regions of the earth.

The contest is not between nations—but between God and Satan. Nations are the "pawns," if you will, of these two great powers. Anywhere the Spirit of God moves, Satan moves to stop Him. God's first move was in the Middle East, among the descendants of Abraham, Isaac, and Jacob. At Pentecost, the Holy Spirit turned to Europe for a harvest among the Gentiles.

Luke records of the First Jerusalem Council following Pentecost: "Simeon hath declared how God at the first did visit the Gentiles to take out of them a people for his name. And to this agree the words of the prophets as it is written" (Acts 15:14-15).

Luke then continues with a statement that defines the regional movement of the Holy Spirit following His Gentile program. "After this I will return, and will build again the tabernacle of David, which is fallen down; and I will build again the ruins thereof, and I will set it up" (Acts 15:16).

In other words, while the Holy Spirit's program was in the Middle East, Satan attempted to set up six world empires in that region—Egypt, Assyria, Babylon, Medopersia, Greece, and Rome. When the Holy Spirit turned to the Gentile world, Satan set up European monarchies that ruled that region with an iron fist for more than a thousand years. Once the times of the Gentiles are finished, God will resume His program with Israel in the Middle East and Satan will raise up a final world leader—the antichrist—to try to stop God from establishing His Son on the throne of Israel and the whole earth forever. Thus, I believe we must rethink the role of the Middle East as we study the origin of the antichrist. Certainly Europe will help to make up Gog's army (see Ezekiel 38 & 39), but the area of focus will be the Middle East.

How Will Antichrist Exhibit His Power?

Paul writes:

> And then the lawless one will be revealed, whom the Lord will consume with the breath of His mouth and destroy with the brightness of His coming. The coming of the lawless one is according to the working of Satan, with all power, signs, and lying wonders, and with all unrighteous deception among those who perish, because they did not receive the love of the truth, that they might be saved. (2 Thessalonians 2:8-10, NKJV)

How will the antichrist exhibit his power? The same way the Christ exhibited His power—in full measure. Whatever evil the political gods of the past have committed, antichrist will do exceedingly more. Whatever great conquests they made, he will excel beyond their record.

Paul said of him, "And then shall that Wicked be revealed... Even him, whose coming is after the working of Satan with all power and signs and lying wonders" (2 Thessalonians 2:8-9).

The antichrist will be a powerful figure. He will perform amazing feats, both natural and supernatural. But his works will be obvious to the saints because they are "lying wonders."

What is a "lying wonder"? It is a superhuman performance that is achieved by a person who does not follow God and His Word in character as well as deed. It is great works—even miracles done in one's own name, to the glory of man and the promotion of evil. By the power of Satan, the antichrist will be a miracle worker who will deceive many—but deceiving none who love the truth.

How Will Antichrist Come to Power?

Daniel says of this man's supernatural powers, "And in the latter time of their kingdom, when the transgressors have reached their fullness, a king shall arise, having fierce features, who understands sinister schemes. His power shall be mighty, but not by his own power..." (Daniel 8:23-24, NKJV). He will be fully empowered by Satan. "...And through his policy also he shall cause craft to prosper in his hand; and he shall magnify himself in his heart, and by peace shall destroy many" (Daniel 8:25).

What was the pattern we observed in the lives of the three famous forerunners of antichrist? They came in as lambs; they went out like wild dogs. Yet it was during their period of peace that they wrapped their airtight cloak of deception around the people and carried them to their destruction.

And what kind of peace ends in destruction? Peace that demands unwise, unsound, ungodly compromise. Hitler first expanded just across the borders into Czechoslovakia. The world said, "We can't go to war for one country." Next went Poland, Hungary, and France. Then bombs began to fall on England. Troops marched into Russia and finally we Americans said, "This is a madman who must be stopped!"

Number One Key to Antichrist's Identity— Extermination of Statehood

But of all the familiar traits the antichrist may exhibit similar to the "lesser antichrists" before him, one feature will be different. The last great world-class leader who is defined in the Scriptures as the antichrist, or the beast, will be a man whose power base is situated eventually in Israel.

After three and one-half years on the high-profile international scene, antichrist is going to set up his headquarters in Israel. At that point he will attack the right of Israel to exist as a nation.

Many people thought that Hitler was the antichrist. But Hitler was in the wrong location and he was only trying to exterminate the Jewish people in Europe. Certainly his hatred of the Jews reflected the "spirit of antichrist," but the beast himself will attack the national existence of the State of Israel. Jeremiah prophesied of that day:

> "For behold, the days are coming," says the Lord, "that I will bring back from captivity My people Israel and Judah," says the Lord. "And I will cause them to return to the land that I gave to their fathers, and they shall possess it." Now these are the words that the Lord spoke concerning Israel and Judah. For thus says the Lord; "We have heard a voice of trembling, of fear, and not of peace. Ask now, and see, whether a man is ever in labor with child? So why do I see every man with his hands on his loins like a woman in labor, and all faces turned pale? Alas! For that day is great, so that none is like it; and it is the time of Jacob's trouble, but he shall be saved out of it." (Jeremiah 30:3-7, NKJV)

Antichrist's Opposition

The antichrist is going to create havoc in the Middle East that will affect the whole world in a way that will make Hitler's work look like a summer outing. The Bible says there has never been a time such as this. However, his madness is not without limitation. The antichrist and the world of the ungodly are not going to be given a *carte blanche*. There will never be a time when God will say to the devil, "Take over." We sometimes forget the fact that even in the worst of times, God is still sovereign. A careful study of the Book of Revelation clearly reveals the empire of antichrist as an increasingly troubled one.

Daniel writes of the antichrist's empire, that it will be loosely knit and troubled by threats of invasion. (See Daniel 11:44).

In a dramatic closing scene, the Bible gives several ways antichrist is going to be hit at the end of his brief seven-year reign, by the power of nature, the Israeli Army, and the Messiah himself:

1.   By the brightness of Jesus coming and His Word (2 Thessalonians 2:8).
2.   By angels. (2 Thessalonians 1:7-10).
3.   By cloudbursts (Ezekiel 38:22).
4.   By great hailstones (Revelation 16:21)
5.   By pestilence and blood (Ezekiel 38:22) .
6.   By the Jewish army (Zechariah 14:14).

Watch out!

The clever, charismatic, world-acclaimed political genius who sets his headquarters up in Israel and declares an end to that nation is suddenly going to be hit with the presence of the greatest government official he as ever encountered. I'm not even sure antichrist is going to recognize Jesus as the Son of God. In fact, I'm sure he will not, because he is going to challenge Jesus for position. But Jesus' words are going to invade the antichrist himself. Then the army of antichrist will be hit with natural disasters, earthquakes, hailstones, and flooding. The angels of God will then empower the Israeli Army, and they will go out as in the days of old, with the strength of David and his slingshot.

In that day the Lord will defend the inhabitants of Jerusalem; the one who is feeble among them in that day shall be like David, and the house of David shall be like God, like the Angel of the Lord before them. It shall be in that day that I will seek to destroy all the nations that come against Jerusalem. (Zechariah 12: 8-9, NKJV)

Antichrist's Final Welcome Party

A welcome party for the antichrist is in the making. The guests have already been invited. Do you want to spy on one of the most interesting scenes that will ever occur in human history? People who doubt the existence of hell, give ear.

On the day the antichrist and his army are destroyed in Israel, hell will be notified. Word will spread from cavern to cavern. "He's coming! Get ready!" Then all the mighty and evil nobles of the past who defied God will gather. Caligula, Nero, great emperors, the Pharaohs, the Caesars, kings, presidents, prime ministers—all will gather in a circle to await the eternal descent of that man who strutted before the cameras of the world, who received the worship of the deceived, who was written up on the front cover of all leading magazines, who held the power of men's lives in his hands without pity. Look at his welcome party on his final arrival home:

Hell from beneath is excited about you, to meet you at your coming; it stirs up the dead for you, all the chief ones of the earth; it has raised up from their thrones all the kings of the nations. They all shall speak and say to you: "Have you also become as weak as we? Have you become like us? Your pomp is brought down to Sheol, and the sound of your stringed instruments; the maggot is spread under you, and worms cover you." (Isaiah 14:9-11, NKJV)

What a fitting ending to such a brilliant career of sin. It is the conclusion to Armageddon. What we want to look at next is the event that follows Armageddon—the Marriage Supper.

9

The Marriage Supper

The Marriage Supper of the Lamb has often been compared to an ancient Jewish wedding where the groom goes away to prepare a place for his bride. At some unexpected moment he suddenly appears at the bride's residence, takes her to the home he has built for her, and for seven days they celebrate with their family and friends.

Many have taken this natural example to mean that the marriage feast between Christ and His saints will be in seclusion in heaven. And while we are enjoying a blissful reunion in that real and glorious city of New Jerusalem, God is going to judge the ungodly world system remaining on earth. Thus, the political, moral, social, and spiritual turmoil man has brought upon himself, described in the Book of Revelation as the Tribulation, will be fulfilled.

The Oriental wedding celebration is perhaps the finest description of what one might expect if God has indeed planned His work according to Jewish tradition. And I believe He has, but not in the sense we have envisioned.

The Marriage Supper of the Lamb is best understood if it is kept in the context in which the Bible places it, which is repeatedly in the midst of a great world-involved war.

Let us go now to the Book of Revelation, where the scene is set. The apostle John is describing the preparation of a great event about to occur:

> And I heard as it were the voice of a great multitude, and as the voice of many waters, and as the voice of mighty thunderings, saying, Alleluia: for the Lord God omnipotent reigneth. Let us be glad and rejoice, and give honour to him: for the marriage of the Lamb is come, and his wife hath made herself ready. And to her was granted that she should be arrayed in fine linen, clean and white: for the fine linen is the righteousness of the saints. And he saith unto me, Write, Blessed are they which are called unto the marriage supper of the Lamb. And he saith unto me, These are the true sayings of God. (Revelation 19:6-9)

What John hears is an announcement in heaven, declaring that the time has come for the Marriage Supper of the Lamb. He is then instructed to write that all who are invited to attend this great feast are blessed.

At this point, one might expect a great gathering of saints from the earth to ascend to the throne where all the wedding preparations are being conducted. But is this the case?

Continuing on with John, let's see what actually follows the announcement that the time has come for the wedding supper.

> And I saw heaven opened, and behold a white horse; and he that sat upon him was called Faithful and True, and in righteousness he doth judge and make war. His eyes were as a flame of fire, and on his head were many crowns; and he had a name written, that no man knew, but he himself. And he was clothed with a vesture dipped in blood: and his name is called The Word of God. And the armies which were in heaven followed him upon white horses, clothed in fine linen, white and clean. (Revelation 19:11-14)

Heaven is preparing for a wedding by sending Jesus down to earth with a massive army? What kind of wedding begins with a war? What kind of groom has an army for attendants? And with whom does the groom intend to do battle?

The Winepress

John answers this in his next statement:

> And out of his [Jesus'] mouth goeth a sharp sword, that with it he should smite the nations: and he shall rule them with a rod of iron: and he treadeth the winepress of the fierceness and wrath of Almighty God. (Revelation 19:15)

The Groom, Jesus, leaves the courts of heaven bound for His wedding supper with a great army prepared to do battle here on earth. The opposing army will be the nations and their godless rulers who have defied the sovereignty of God. (It will be an army of demon-energized people.) I watched a congresswoman arguing her case for abortion before nationwide television. As she did so, she took God's name in vain with a vileness that would put legs back on the serpent himself.

And I was reminded once again of the arrogance of end-times people on their way to Armageddon.

John calls the actual location of this end-time battleground a "winepress." And although all nations will be represented at this historic site, the war itself will not be an earth-wide invasion from heaven. Jesus and His army will target only one specific location. It is a spot Ezekiel clearly identified some 600 years earlier when he spoke by inspiration of the Spirit:

> And, thou son of man, thus saith the Lord God; Speak unto every feathered fowl, and to every beast of the field, Assemble yourselves, and come; gather yourselves on every side to my sacrifice that I do sacrifice for you, even a great sacrifice upon the mountains of Israel, that ye may eat flesh, and drink blood. (Ezekiel 39:17)

The "winepress," the place of battle which Jesus shall address at His Second Coming to earth, is the land of Israel. Jesus is coming to Israel to do battle. It is in Israel that the Wedding Supper of the Lamb occurs.

As I have stated already, contrary to popular notion, I do not believe that the Marriage Supper of Christ and His saints will take place in one of the desirable gardens of heaven. God commanded Ezekiel to speak to every feathered fowl and wild beast of earth to gather in the land of Israel for His future nuptial banquet:

> Ye shall eat the flesh of the mighty, and drink the blood of the princes of the earth, of rams, of lambs, and of goats, of bullocks, all of them fatlings of Bashan. And ye shall eat fat till ye be full, and drink blood till ye be drunken, of my sacrifice which I have sacrificed for you. Thus ye shall be filled at my table with horses and chariots, with mighty men, and with all men of war, saith the Lord of God. (Ezekiel 39:18-20)

The Last Great Invasion

A future battle is coming in the land of Israel where the blood of the fallen is going to become food for an influx of birds and animals such as man has never seen. It will be a divine ingathering of wildlife brought about by a supernatural summons. Jesus described it as "the carcass" where the eagles would be gathered together (See Matthew 24:28).

Job heard it; Ezekiel prophesied it. (See Ezekiel 39:18-20.) John saw it:

> And I saw an angel standing in the sun; and he cried with a loud voice, saying to all the fowls that fly in the midst of heaven, Come and gather yourselves together unto the supper of the great God; That ye may eat the flesh of kings, and the flesh of captains, and the flesh of mighty men, and the flesh of horses, and of them that sit on them, and the flesh of all men, both free and bond, both small and great. (Revelation 19:17-18)

The menu for the wild-life at the Marriage Supper of the Lamb of God will be the bodies of the rebels who fall in battle during the last great invasion of Israel.

But the Scriptures are even more specific. We not only know that the marriage will be held on earth, in the land of Israel, we also know its precise location.

The Prophet Joel declared:

> Proclaim ye this among the Gentiles; Prepare war, wake up the mighty men, let all the men of war draw near, let them come up: Beat your plowshares into swords, and your pruninghooks into spears: let the weak say, I am strong. Assemble yourselves, and come, all ye heathen, and gather yourselves together round about: thither cause thy mighty

95

> ones to come down, O Lord. Let the heathen be wakened, and come up to the valley of Jehoshaphat: for there will I sit to judge all the heathen round about. (Joel 3:9-12)

"Jehoshaphat" is another name for the Valley of Megiddo (Armageddon), a site about fifty-seven miles outside the city of Jerusalem in Israel. John also confirms this predicted location in his Revelation:

> Behold, I come as a thief. Blessed is he that watcheth, and keepeth his garments, lest he walk naked, and they see his shame. And he gathered them together into a place called in the Hebrew tongue Armageddon. (Revelation 16:15-16)

The Valley of Armageddon, in the land of Israel, is the table which God will use to serve the guests which have been invited to attend His Son's wedding supper.

Jesus' First Miracle

The first miracle Jesus performed on earth was at a wedding in Cana. Not far from Cana, Jesus will one day come again to perform an even greater miracle. Whereas at Cana, Jesus converted a few pots of water into the finest wine ever tasted, at Armageddon Jesus is going to convert a 186-mile long-valley of blood into wine for the birds and animals where they will drink until they have become intoxicated with His miracle. Napoleon called this valley the greatest natural battlefield in the world. It is estimated to be able to accommodate four hundred million soldiers.

The flow of blood from those fallen in battle is what causes Armageddon to be repeatedly called a "winepress." An ancient winepress is where the grapes were gathered into a large vat and trampled by human feet until the juice of the grapes had fully surrendered. And "surrender" will be the whole point of Jesus' sudden return to our beleaguered, war-torn planet.

When Jesus sets His feet on the Mount of Olives, there will be a major war ensuing in the city of Jerusalem as well as in the Valley of Armageddon. The threat of Israel's annihilation is the catalyst that prompts God into action. Read it in the words of Zechariah the prophet:

> Behold, the day of the Lord cometh, and thy spoil shall be divided in the midst of thee. For I will gather all nations against Jerusalem to battle; and the city shall be taken, and the houses rifled, and the women ravished; and half of the city shall go forth into captivity, and the residue of the people shall not be cut off from the city. Then shall the Lord go forth, and fight against those nations, as when he fought in the day of battle. And his feet shall stand in that day upon the mount of Olives, which is before Jerusalem on the east, and the mount of Olives shall cleave in the midst thereof toward the east and toward the west, and there shall be a very great valley; and half of the mountain shall remove toward the north, and half of it toward the south.... and the Lord my God shall come, and all the saints with thee. (Zechariah 14:1-5)

The moment Jesus' feet touch the earth, there will be a major earthquake. The mountains and valleys in Israel will undergo radical, physical changes. No doubt this earthquake will get the attention of those battling a few miles away, in the Valley of Armageddon—where Jesus will be advancing from Jerusalem.

Jesus Confronts Antichrist

Upon Jesus' arrival at Armageddon, He will confront the army of the great world leader in the Middle East. Antichrist, as we have seen, is the world-class leader who has gained international respect and cooperation. Operating in the role of negotiator for peace in the Middle East, the antichrist will have convinced the leaders of all powerful nations that the Jews must give up the land of Israel for the sake of world harmony. Israel's resistance to this plan will have sparked the battles raging in Jerusalem and the Valley of Armageddon, when Jesus arrives. And according to Isaiah, no nation will be standing with Israel in this battle.

> Who is this that cometh from Edom, from the city of Bozrah, with his magnificent garments of crimson? Who is this in kingly robes, marching in the greatness of his strength? "It is I, the Lord, announcing your salvation; I, the Lord, the one who is mighty to save!" "Why are your clothes so red, as from treading out the grapes?" "I have trodden the winepress alone. No one was there to help me. In my wrath I have trodden my enemies like grapes. In my fury I trampled my foes. It is their blood you see upon my clothes. For the time has come for me to avenge my people [Israel], to redeem them from the hands of their oppressors. I looked but no one came to help them; I was amazed and appalled. So I executed vengeance alone; unaided, I meted out judgment. I crushed the heathen nations in my anger and made them stagger and fall to the ground. (Isaiah 63:1-6, The Book)

Jesus is that man from Bozrah whose garments are splattered with blood. Israel is the people He has come to rescue single-handedly. Armageddon is the "winepress of the wrath of God" where the pride of man confronts the end of God's patience with rebellion.

Israel—Jesus' Residence

And with this revelation, the whole picture begins to make sense. The Wedding Supper of Christ will be held at His residence, as ancient Jewish custom predicts. It is an error to think that Jesus will reside in the distant heavens forever. He is coming down to Israel. Listen once again to what Gabriel, who stands in the very presence of God, said to Mary:

> And in the sixth month the angel Gabriel was sent from God unto a city of Galilee, named Nazareth. ...And the angel said unto her, Fear not, Mary: for thou hast found favour with God. And, behold, thou shalt conceive in thy womb, and bring forth a son, and shalt call his name JESUS. He shall be great, and shall be called the Son of the Highest: and the Lord God shall give unto him the throne of his father David: And he shall reign over the house of Jacob for ever; and of his kingdom there shall be no end. (Luke 1:26, 30-33)

Following this, after 1,000 years of clean up, New Jerusalem is coming down into the sphere of planet earth. A "planet" will relocate. Forever the nation of Israel is going to inhabit the land of Israel. The world's ignorance of this fact is the cause of the present trouble in the Middle East.

The Ultimate Wedding Feast

The Marriage Supper begins with God standing and blowing a trumpet, followed by Gabriel calling with a loud voice. At that moment, the atmosphere between heaven and earth will roll back like a scroll. John described it as heaven being "opened."

On spirit horses, such as angels ride (see Revelation 6), Jesus, the angels, and the saints who have been caught up to meet the Lord in the air will descend where the "carcass of war" is in a life-and-death struggle. Israel will win or die in that day. Satan himself will triumph or lose. Love and hate will be locked in mortal combat. But King Jesus, the King of kings [spiritual kings—His saints, as well as rulers of natural kingdoms] will descend upon the scene. And amazing as it may seem, the evil, Satan-possessed antichrist will turn and attempt to destroy the Son of God himself. John said:

> And I saw the beast, and the kings of the earth, and their armies, gathered together to make war against him that sat on the horse, and against his army. And the beast was taken, and with him the false prophet that wrought miracles before him, with which he deceived them that had received the mark of the beast, and them that worshipped his image. These both were cast alive into a lake of fire burning with brimstone. And the remnant were slain with the sword of him that sat upon the horse, which sword proceeded out of his mouth: and all the fowls were filled with their flesh. (Revelation 19:19-21)

That is feasting! This is God's idea of a real celebration. The ultimate in dining is not steak and strawberries. Divine feasting is the ultimate and final triumph of God over Satan, good over evil, truth over error, the righteous over the wicked, faith over unbelief, God's Word over the intellectual wasteland of human logic!

There has never been an event to compare with the Marriage Supper of the Lamb. Remember the words Jesus once declared to His disciples, "My meat is to do the will of him that sent me" (John 4:34). There is a food for the eternal soul that satisfies the taste buds of the heart far beyond anything the natural palate has ever tasted. It is called victory!

Without question, all the saints of God could not be seated, as we envision seating, around a white linen table even if it were the length of the nation of Israel. I suspect the innumerable hosts of saints at the Marriage Supper will be suspended just above the Valley of Decision, with a clear view of everything that is being served on "The Great Day of the Lord" menu. We shall feast with the eyes of our soul, on the ultimate victory of the Word of God (the same powerful Word that is available to us now), and our souls shall be satisfied with a sight that is presently revealed only in part to us.

What a moment! What a celebration! What a banquet to anticipate! Only a fool would not want to be on the winning side! This is not to say that we will not sit down with our Lord in the Millennium and eat real food. The Scriptures are clear that the saints will sit together at His table. Jesus said, "But I say to you, I will not drink of this fruit of the vine from now on until that day when I drink it new with you in My Father's kingdom" (Matthew 26:29, NKJV). But the greatest bread we will ever taste will be the joint venture of the Spirit we will take with our Lord and Savior Jesus.

When, Where, Why

When will the Marriage Supper of the Lamb take place? It will begin at the Second Coming of Jesus. This period of time, which began with the Judgement of God being poured out on the sins of the nations some three-and-a-half years earlier, is called in the Scriptures the "Day of the Lord" or the "Great Day of God." It is quite possible the Day of the

Lord will last for the 1,000-year millennial restoration. And only at the end of the Millennium, when all powers have been made subject to Christ, will New Jerusalem be the Bride, come down out of heaven for the final nuptial feasting.

Where will the marriage supper take place? In the land of Israel.

Why will it occur?

1. To celebrate the final defeat of Satan and his followers.

2. To deliver the nation of Israel from all its enemies externally and all its sin internally—and to reveal its Messiah.

3. To witness to the heathen nations who remain on earth after the Tribulation, that there is one God and His eternal Son, Jesus, who is appointed Lord over all. It will be a witness which is certain to spark a great world-wide conversion of those held in bondage to false religions. I believe this will be the greatest revival, or ingathering, the earth has ever experienced.

4. Finally, it will be that moment when we will sit down with the patriarchs, our loved ones, and our Lord for a meal that will initiate the beginnings of eternity.

The world system is falling apart. Men are looking for a deliverer. But Jesus told us plainly that there will be no lasting peace, no lasting answers, until He comes again.

In the next chapter we shall discuss His Second Coming as it is declared in the famous Parable of the Ten Virgins.

10

The Parable of the Ten Virgins

Ten, in biblical numerics, is the number of perfection. Ten was the number required to form a synagogue, or to be present at any formal ceremony or benediction. According to Talmudic authorities, ten lamps were used in a bridal procession. We might, therefore, take Jesus' use of ten virgins to mean that this parable has all the elements of a perfect picture of the coming kingdom. For this reason, let us take a moment to read the full story.

> Then the kingdom of heaven shall be likened to ten virgins who took their lamps and went out to meet the bridegroom. Now five of them were wise, and five were foolish. Those who were foolish took their lamps and took no oil with them, but the wise took oil in their vessels with their lamps. But while the bridegroom was delayed, they all slumbered and slept. And at midnight a cry was heard: "Behold, the bridegroom is coming; go out to meet him!" Then all those virgins arose and trimmed their lamps. And the foolish said to the wise, "Give us some of your oil, for our lamps are going out." But the wise

answered, saying, "No, lest there should not be enough for us and you; but go rather to those who sell, and buy for yourselves." And while they went to buy, the bridegroom came, and those who were ready went in with him to the wedding; and the door was shut. Afterward the other virgins came also, saying, "Lord, Lord, open to us!" But he answered and said, "Assuredly, I say to you, I do not know you." Watch therefore, for you know neither the day nor the hour in which the Son of Man is coming. (Matthew 25:1-13, NKJV)

If we go back to the first line of this parable, it becomes obvious that the theme of Jesus' message is not ten virgins. His opening statement makes it clear that He is talking about the Kingdom of Heaven. "Then the kingdom of heaven shall be likened to ten virgins who took their lamps and went out to meet the bridegroom" (vs. 1).

The subject is the Kingdom. The metaphor used to talk about the kingdom is a wedding—an ancient Jewish wedding.

A Brief Pattern of an Ancient Jewish Wedding:

• The bridegroom with his party leaves his home for the bride's residence.

• Upon hearing the sound of the bridegroom coming, the bride sends out virgins to greet him.

• Ultimately the bride joins the groom and they go to his residence—where she is unveiled and presented to him for the consummation of the marriage.

A Western Christian Wedding (essentially the same pattern):

• The Church is set. The bride's party waits outside for the arrival of the groom at the altar.

• The groom and his party arrives at the altar.

• The bridesmaids (virgins) go down to meet them.

• Finally the bride comes down the aisle, joins the groom, and is unveiled for the ceremony.

The Bridegroom of the Parable of the Ten Virgins is clearly Jesus. He appears in the clouds to gather the saints to himself. The saints include the bodily resurrection of all believing dead, along with all living believers on earth at the time of Christ's appearing in the heavens.

> For this we say to you by the word of the Lord, that we who are alive and remain until the coming of the Lord will by no means precede those who are asleep. For the Lord Himself will descend from heaven with a shout, with the voice of an archangel, and with the trumpet of God. And the dead in Christ will rise first. Then we who are alive and remain shall be caught up together with them in the clouds to meet the Lord in the air. And thus we shall always be with the Lord. (1 Thessalonians 4:15-17, NKJV)

This is commonly known as the Rapture. In the Parable of the Ten Virgins, the Rapture occurs when the Bridegroom Jesus appears in the clouds. The "virgins" are part of the bridal party. The five who are caught up are those who truly know the Bridegroom. The five who are careless miss out. I do not believe we should complicate the role of the virgins beyond this. It is a warning to the Church in every generation to be ready for the Lord's appearing.

But look again at this parable and ask yourself who is missing. What key person is only alluded to indirectly? Where is the bride in this setting? The Groom is there with His party. The bridesmaids are there, but how does the bride fit in? To be more specific, who is the Bride of Christ? That is what we are going to investigate in these next few pages.

The first man, Adam, had his wife chosen for him. God gave Eve to Adam. The second man, Adam (Jesus), has His wife chosen for Him. God has promised a choice bride as His Son's eternal companion. And down through the ages, fathers have kept the pattern alive, especially in the East, by securing wives for their sons. The pattern that began in heaven is on the earth. It is here as a witness to the fact of the eternal marriage that is coming between the Son of God and His bride.

The bigger view of life makes it clear that a permanent covenant between Christ and His inheritance was the plan from the beginning. A marriage is a covenant between two parties. At the end of the Millennial Reign of Christ on the earth, Jesus will enter into an eternal relationship with the bride for whom He paid such a great price.

The writer of Hebrews says, "...Jesus, the author and finisher of our faith, who for the joy that was set before Him endured the cross, despising the shame..." (Hebrews, 12:2 NKJV). In order to inherit all things that were determined for Him from the beginning, Jesus paid a price greater than man can possibly appreciate. It was a price that included total humiliation of the Creator before His creation.

A reputable, but overly confident doctor appeared before national cameras and boldly declared a young athlete with a heart problem able to continue playing his game. "It is up to us to monitor his heart and keep him safe!" he said with an almost God-like assurance. In less than six months that young athlete died on a basketball court, and the doctor suffered national professional embarrassment.

A few years ago, with millions of viewers watching, a baseball player missed the score that would have won his team the national pennant. A short time later he committed suicide.

On landing his passenger airliner, a Japanese pilot wrecked his craft. Humiliated before his country, he too ended his life.

In a thousand ways each day we are reminded of the intense pain of public embarrassment and shame. Public knowledge of a personal failure is difficult to bear. But if all the embarrassment of the human race were put together in one big mass, it would not compare to the shame suffered by the Son of God at His rejection by His own creation. As flawed people, sooner or later, we forgive the failures of others. But the flawless Son of God endured total rejection by flawed people, because He did a perfect work for those who are imperfect.

The Son of God left the courts of heaven with all creation peering down. Innocent God came down to guilty man, offered himself for man's guilt, and was officially rejected. We could say that guilty man slapped the face of innocent God, and Jesus allowed it because of the joy He would eventually possess. The bride would one day become His if He endured the humiliation of the cross. Before the great hosts of powerful angels and worshiping lords of heaven; before millions of screeching, jeering, shaggy demons, and demonic princes of Satan; before proud, vain little man in his moment of glory, Jesus would win His bride if He kept His eye on the guaranteed joy. And what a bride she must be in His eyes to pay such a price! Of all the things He could have taken as His inheritance, Jesus paid with His own life to obtain the bride. What must she be like? What beauty must she possess! What value! In these closing pages, this is what we want to discover. Who is the Bride of Christ? What is her destiny and how does that affect our lives today?

Since the when day Adam and Eve rebelled, the world has been living under a corrupt political and religious system. Even though God sent a flood to destroy these two evil systems, within 100 years Noah's great-grandson Nimrod had picked up Satan's mandate in Babylon, the very place where Adam and Eve fell, and he began to reseed the earth once again with false worship and government. Babylon is the womb of every false religion that is on the earth today. The rampant moral evils, the violence, the greed, all false worship originated in ancient Babylonia about 4,500 years ago. Sin is old, seasoned, and very clever. It is the catalyst that will bring about divine judgments described in Revelation 17 and 18.

In the Revelation, John got a divine preview of the ungodly religions and political systems that have empowered each other since Nimrod. The title of these systems is "Mystery Babylon the Great, the Mother of Harlots and Abominations of the Earth." Greed for money is the power of sin. (See Revelation 17:5). John saw the whole financial and religious structure of the nations totally collapse. Following this collapse, he witnesses another scene. This one takes place in heaven:

> After these things I heard a loud voice of a great multitude in heaven, saying, "Alleluia! Salvation and glory and honor belong to the Lord our God! For true and righteous are His judgments, because He has judged the great harlot who corrupted the earth with her fornication; and He has avenged on her the blood of His servants shed by her." (Reveleation 19:1-2, NKJV)

This great voice of the people in heaven goes on to say,

> Let us be glad and rejoice and give Him glory, for the marriage of the Lamb has come, and His wife has made herself ready. And to her it was granted to be arrayed in fine linen, clean and bright, for the fine linen is the righteous acts of the saints. Then he said to me, "Write: 'Blessed are those who are called to the marriage supper of the Lamb!'" (Revelation 19:7-9, NKJV)

Who is the Bride of Christ? For years the best answer the Church could give was itself. The Church alone is the Bride of Christ. But further investigation into the Scriptures gives the Bride a much greater identity. Although the Church is a part of the Bride, it is much more than the Church.

Who is the Bride?

Let us join John now as he describes the Bride:

> Then I, John, saw the holy city, New Jerusalem, coming down out of heaven from God, prepared as a bride adorned for her husband. And I heard a loud voice from heaven saying, "Behold, the tabernacle of God is with men, and He will dwell with them, and they shall be His people, and God Himself will be with them and be their God." (Revelation 21:2-3 NKJV)

As if this were not sufficient confirmation, an angel also appears to John with this clear statement:

"Come hither, I will shew thee the bride, the Lamb's wife." And he carried me away in the spirit to a great and high mountain, and shewed me that great city, the holy Jerusalem, descending out of heaven from God. Having the glory of God: and her light was like a stone most precious, even like a jasper stone, clear as crystal. (Revelation 21:9-10)

Without question, the Bride of Christ is New Jerusalem.

From the day when God first called Abraham out of Babylonia, Abraham stated his quest. He was in search of the "city which hath foundations, whose builder and maker [architect] is God" (Hebrews 11:10). Abraham was looking for the Bride of Christ.

Unlike any other city of creation, New Jerusalem is unique. Men have built the great cities we love to visit and admire in the various countries today. But New Jerusalem is a city with a spiritual foundation. It is built on the truth preached by the Apostles and Prophets of Jesus Christ (See Ephesians 2:20). The Bride of Christ, New Jerusalem, is a city built on a foundation that will never crumble. "Heaven and earth shall pass away: but my words shall not pass away" (Mark 13:31).

The crisis of inner-city decay is rampant worldwide in the kingdom of men. Not so in the Bride of Christ. Her core is only gaining in strength and beauty. "Let us be glad and rejoice and give Him glory, for the marriage of the Lamb has come, and His wife has made herself ready" (Revelation 19:7).

Landmarks in New Jerusalem

For 6,000 years of human history, while the world systems have been running their course, Christ has been building and decorating His bride—the New Jerusalem. The non-person materials of the buildings, streets, and foundations of this city are made out of the most precious metals and gems in all creation.

The city was pure gold....And the twelve gates were twelve pearls and the street of the city was pure gold... (Revelation 21:18-21)

But look at what else it says about the gates and foundations of this special city. Not only are the materials used to construct them of inestimable value, they are named after real people from the earth.

> Her light was like unto a stone most precious, even like a jasper stone, clear as crystal; And had a wall great and high, and had twelve gates... and names written thereon, which are the names of the twelve tribes of the children of Israel... And the wall of the city had twelve foundations, and in them the names of the twelve apostles of the Lamb!"
> (Revelation 21:11-14)

Stop and think about the possibility of this statement. If the walls and foundations are named for human beings, this may well mean that just as we name boulevards, streets, parks, and buildings after men, so Jesus has named places for the honorable saints on earth.

Revelation 19:7-8 reads:

> Let us be glad and rejoice, and give honour to him: for the arriage of the Lamb is come, and his wife hath made herself ready. And to her was granted that she should be arrayed in fine linen, clean and white: for the fine linen is the righteousness of saints.

Who knows the countless righteous acts that may be acknowledged inside New Jerusalem,—and what form they may take? Famous saints, unknown saints, anyone who has distinguished himself in this life by denying himself so that God might be glorified, may well find his name inscribed in New Jerusalem.

Think of it. Millions of men and women have sold their souls to have their names immortalized in the notable places of this present world. What an honor to be written up in history. But how much more honorable to be written in the books of heaven, placed in the libraries of New Jerusalem for saints to read throughout eternity! How much more honorable to have a park or a building named for you in New Jerusalem than the crumbling cities that Satan offered to Jesus if He would forget about God's Kingdom!

The glory of this world is quickly passing away. All those who have given everything for its fleeting glories are going to fade painfully with it. Most will be lost. None will have the glory that rightfully belonged to them. Believers who loved this present world more than God will enter the Holy City with nothing but their souls and a place to live.

> Each one's work will become clear; for the Day will declare it, because it will be revealed by fire; and the fire will test each one's work, of what sort it is. If anyone's work which he has built on it endures, he will receive a reward. If anyone's work is burned, he will suffer loss; but he himself will be saved, yet so as through fire. (1 Corinthians 3:13-15, NKJV)

The art, the beauty, the momentary pleasures of this world's careers have peaked. The upward spiral of civilization has turned downward. We are regressing toward thoughtless, uncivilized behavior. Life has lost its artistry. It is getting set to be replaced by a glory that will go on with increasing beauty and divine unfoldings forever. Paul referred to it as "glory rolling in upon glory."

The physical features of New Jerusalem are glorious, as we have seen. But what about its spiritual buildings? The Bride of Christ is not just magnificent buildings, gems, and precious metals, she is a city decorated with the best of people—men and women who resisted the persecutions and lusts of this present world in order to build the Holy City. Yes, in the midst of the dazzling city of treasures, are billions upon billions of radiant souls totally transformed into divine temples—filled with the Spirit of the living God. "Know ye not that ye are the temple of God, and that the Spirit of God dwelleth in you?" (1 Corinthinians 3:16).

Imagine living in a community of perfect human beings, totally transformed into loving, humble, worshiping, just, completely productive people. Without question, New Jerusalem will not only have buildings gilded with every precious stone imaginable, but this city will be the political answer to national and international peace and productivity forever.

> And the nations of those who are saved [during the millennial reign of Christ on earth for 1,000 years] shall walk in its [New Jerusalem's] light [wisdom and counsel], and the kings of the earth [regenerated, natural people] do bring their glory and honor into it. ...But there shall by no means enter it anything that defiles, or causes an abomination or a lie, but only those who are written in the Lamb's Book of Life. (Revelation 21:24-27, NKJV)

When Christ, "the Bridegroom," appears in the clouds to rapture the "Virgins" (the saints, past and present) then will come the Judgment Seat of Christ, where believers are purged of all "spots and wrinkles." Awards and kingdom positions will be assigned. The saints will then proceed from the heavens to earth. Satan will be bound. Restoration will begin. Old Testament saints will rise to the occasion of their original mandate. Israel will become a kingdom of priests and a spiritual light for the nations as God first intended them to be. The Church will spread out over the Gentile nations to bring about the restoration of their entire social, moral, and spiritual life. All will be serving under Christ, the King, reigning in Jerusalem. There will be both immortal saints and eternal natural people on the earth working together to restore the earth to its original Edenic State.

After 1,000 years of purifying, cleansing, and beautifying the earth, Satan will be permanently dealt with and cast into hell forever, along with any rebels remaining on the earth (See Revelation 20). Unbelievers will be resurrected, judged, and sentenced to eternal separation from God, in varying degrees of hell.

Eternity will then appear on the horizon. All creation will lift up its eyes, and coming down the aisles of space will be the Bride—New Jerusalem—the eternal home of all the saints who trusted in God before Jesus' Second Coming to earth. All the beauty, the light, the wealth of divine imagination will be represented in this most glorious realm of all creation. No city, no planet, no simple deposit of wealth, however great, will begin to compare with the glorious bride which the Groom himself designed and built by His own sacrificial greatness.

Nothing man has ever possessed will compare to citizenship in this glistening Holy City. It will be the supreme agony of all who miss it. "There will be weeping and gnashing of teeth, when you see Abraham and Isaac and Jacob and all the prophets in the kingdom of God, and yourselves thrust out" (Luke 13:28, NKJV). It will be the unfulfilled desire of the natural generations who were saved during the Millennium, after the Coming of Jesus. But only those who have trusted in Christ before He comes again will possess this treasured citizenship. Natural people will be able to visit the Holy City and bring the gifts of their labors from earth, just as ancient kings come laden with wealth to honor Solomon, but they will never be allowed to live in the City of the Great King. (See Revelation 21:24.) This distinction belongs only to the saints who were ready at the sound of the trumpet. Surely this will be the fulfilling of the words spoken by the Queen of Sheba, when she said to the first King Solomon, who was a type of Christ and His coming kingdom. "...Indeed the half was not told to me. Your wisdom and prosperity exceed the fame of which I heard" (1 Kings 10:7, NKJV).

New Jerusalem encompasses 1,500 square miles. It is as tall as it is long. That is a distance from Florida to Maine, and every inch will be a landmark of the righteous deeds of those who sacrificed this present world's attractions that they might live in the eternal kingdom. But beyond its physical beauty, beyond the adornment of the righteous deeds of the saints, there is a majesty awaiting in New Jerusalem that is unspeakable and full of glory. It is the focus of all creation; the nucleus of every atom; the longing of every emotion; the wisdom of every intellect; the first cause of all causes. In the midst of the Bride of Christ, enthroned in His own indefinable majesty, willbe the presence of the great God and our Father coming down to tabernacle among men.

One day at the end of the Millennial Reign of Christ, when He has brought every power into submission to God, New Jerusalem will come down out of heaven to earth. In that day Jesus will offer a totally submissive earth and creation back to the God and Father of all. God will, in turn, reward Jesus for His great sacrificial work by giving Him the Holy City, its hosts of angels, its redeemed and battle-proven saints as His possession. Together we shall worship and celebrate and build and expand throughout unlimited space forever!

11

The Restoration of All Things

The focal point of any orchestra is the conductor. The man in the first chair may perform magnificently; the man in the last chair may get out of tune. In either case, the orchestra will follow neither of the two men. Although other members may be affected when one gets out of tune, each musician is responsible for his own performance by keeping his eye on the conductor. The earth is made up of a symphony of nations. Regardless of size, each is important, each has a role to play, but the conductor will never relinquish the focus from center stage. Ultimately, all eyes will go back to the man with the baton.

According to history, our present civilization began in the Middle East. Eden was located somewhere in the Tigris-Euphrates region known as modern-day Iraq. After the Flood—when all living people and animals were drowned except Noah, his family, and the animals they preserved—Noah's Ark landed again in that same region of earth on Mt. Ararat (Armenia and Turkey) and once again nations began to spread from the Middle Eastern area.

Only a faint knowledge of geography will immediately draw a circle around one central spot of earth, and we soon discover that all six of the history-shaping empires of the world were birthed in this one general location. Egypt, Assyria, Babylon, Medo-Persia, Greece, and Rome are situated in the Middle East-Mediterranean area.

About 3,400 years after Adam and Eve had been driven from the Garden of Eden, a prophet named Daniel had a dream from God. The Egyptian Empire had come and gone; the Assyrian Empire was on the other side of its glory. Now Daniel saw the image of a man with a head of gold which represented the present great Babylonian Empire in which Daniel lived. The breast of the image was silver and represented the coming Medo-Persian Empire. The trunk and thighs of brass represented the Grecian Empire under Alexander the Great, and the legs of iron represented the future Roman Empire, at the first and second coming of Messiah. We know from history that the Roman Empire eventually divided into two parts. The eastern section, with its capital at Constantinople, and the western, with its capital at Rome. One leg of the eastern empire has ultimately become the Islamic world of the Middle East (with tiny Israel in it); and one leg of the western empire has ultimately become a portion of Christian Europe down to the coast of the Mediterranean. There is no mistaking it, Daniel's image was standing squarely in the Middle East with one leg reaching into a portion of Europe and the Mediterranean.

And now, some 2,500 years later, we know that Daniel was one hundred percent correct in what he recorded. With complete accuracy, His vision pinpointed the birth of the major world powers that have most significantly affected the course of divine history.

Every nation stands in the shadow of the cradle of civilization. China once enjoyed great dynasties but they did not conquer the world, nor did they influence its religious ideologies outside their own region to any significant degree. India boasted of vast wealth in gold and silks, but they did not conquer the world nor significantly influence its thinking. Great Britain, perhaps the greatest empire of this era, greatly influenced the world with both western and Christian culture, yet God did not include them in His history-shaping image.

The scientist who conducted the discoveries of the sunken *Bismarck* and *Titanic* was interviewed about his explorations of the trade route between Rome and Carthage. About the Mediterranean Sea, the scientist had this to say: "This body of water contains more history than all the museums of earth combined."

The symphony of nations has been underway for almost 6,000 years. God is not going to change the conductor. Daniel's man stood in the Middle East with one leg reaching into the Euro-Mediterranean region. The Middle East is center stage from which the course of history has been and will continue to be conducted, even after Jesus arrives in Jerusalem to establish divine government upon the earth.

This does not mean that only the Mediterranean and the Middle East are important. Jesus died for souls in every nation. The Holy Spirit is on the earth, reaching out to every place and person who will respond to His voice; and each nation is held accountable for its response. Yet, the fact remains that history is being directed from one region.

Consider that in the Middle Eastern area:
- Today's civilization was born.
- God made His first covenant with man (Abraham).
- The six world empires of the Scriptures were birthed.
- All the prophets, who foretold the coming of Messiah and the destiny of the world, were born and lived there.
- Jesus, the Messiah, was born in this region.
- God birthed the New Covenant Church in the Middle East.
- The Bible was written there.
- The Holy Spirit fell there.
- Israel ceased as a nation there, only to be revived almost 2,000 years later—something no other nation has ever done.
- The last great war is predicted there, in the Valley of Armageddon.
- Jesus promised to return to this region and establish His headquarters as King of all nations.
- The nations of the earth will be ruled from the Middle East during the Millennium. According to sociologists, the four major religions of the world are Hinduism, Buddhism, Islam, and Christianity. Ask yourself, how does Buddha fit into the hub of this wheel of human development and destiny? How do the multi-gods of Hinduism fit into this picture? How does Muhammad, with his personal definition of god, Allah, and his one-man philosophy of himself as the final prophet, fit into the Mediterranean story?

Twentieth-century man has the benefit of stepping back and considering the whole picture. Thousands of years have gone by. Which of these religions is a believable part of *real history?*

The first coming of Jesus is a historical fact. Both secular and religious historians record the fact of a man named Jesus, who claimed to have been sent from God to save man from his sins. Unfortunately the people who compare Jesus with other religious leaders stop here. They compare the good works and good words of all religious leaders and conclude "six in one, half dozen in the other." But Jesus' first coming is only half of His story.

With the exception of Jesus, all other religious men and ideologies promise a better place *somewhere* else. Even reincarnation eventually hopes to arrive at a glorious state of nirvana. But no religious leader promises to return to this earth and blanket the whole natural, social, political and religious system until everything is completely healed on this planet.

Only Jesus promises the one thing the world really needs. The atmosphere doesn't need religion—it needs to be delivered of its smog. Wild animals don't need religion—they need to be delivered of the killing instinct. Rivers and oceans don't need religion—they need to be delivered from man's pollution. And man doesn't need religion—he needs *total restoration*. He needs to be restored to a spiritual, moral, and physical state that he is unable to achieve on his own.

We fight disease with medicine, but we never quite conquer all sickness. We fight injustice with law, but we can never quite close our courts and tell the police force to go home. The whole earth is plagued with a curse from which it needs to be cleansed. Most religions have had thousands of years to do the job, but they have hardly made a dent. This is why Jesus is the only hope of such a salvation.

Jesus' *first coming* to earth demonstrated the power of God to exercise authority over creation. Jesus' *crucifixion* at Calvary demonstrated the power of God to confront man's great curse—sin. Jesus' *resurrection* demonstrated the power of God over man's great enemy—death. And Jesus' *ascension* demonstrated God's preparations for the final stage of earthwide restoration.

Christianity has not corrected all the ills of the earth. We do not have a world-saving mandate. The world system is condemned to death and all those who follow it.

> For Moses truly said to the fathers, "The Lord your God will raise up for you a Prophet like me from your brethren. Him you shall hear in all things, whatever He says to you. And it shall be that every soul who will not hear that Prophet shall be utterly destroyed from among the people." (Acts 3:22-23, NKJV)

It makes sense to attempt to preserve this beautiful earth as best we can for the health of future generations. It makes sense to work for peace. But healing for the earth and all nations of people is yet to be accomplished. Certainly no thinking person would say that we are anywhere near peace and restoration at this point.

The penalty of sin was paid at Calvary. With that payment, the power of sin was broken. But the salvation of all things will not be fully realized until Jesus returns to enforce the job He accomplished at Calvary. If you have ever wondered why the Church doesn't seem to provide all the answers to the world's ills, it will, when the Lord of the Church returns to conduct the final restoration.

Jesus is coming again, and that's one major thing that distinguishes Him from all other religious leaders. Buddha, Muhammad, and any other religious notables did whatever they were going to do for the earth while they were here. But not one of them will be back to do anything more. They are dead to the events of this earth forever. They each left behind their philosophy, but they will not return to see how it's working. They are finished, except as individuals who will one day stand before God and give an account of their relationship to the true picture.

Every nation has enthroned its religion and romanticized its culture. We each see our culture as center stage. But we need to get our eyes back on the Conductor. Millions of souls could have been saved if man had just viewed history accurately. Millions can be saved today if we can get them to view the world scene according to the real picture. The focus of world history is the Middle East.

Abraham had many sons, but only one son received the mandate to produce the Savior of the world. Isaac fathered Jacob; Jacob fathered Judah; Judah fathered the line from which came David. And from David came Messiah, Yeshua (Jesus). Everything, all cultures, all religions, all national interests will one day bow to the baton of Jesus.

In the next chapter, we will examine eight proofs as to why Jesus alone qualifies to rule the world.

12

Who Will Rule the World?

The great religious divisions on the earth do not exist because of the possibility of the existence of God. Most of the world has always understood that desire for God is not merely a taught behavior. Great religious divisions come when men try to agree on the person God has chosen to represent Him here on earth. This will be our present subject for discussion.

In this chapter, I am going to offer evidence that will seek to prove the right of only one person to mediate between God and the human race. I believe this man is the one leader capable of assuming the throne of world government, and He is, in fact, God's only answer to world peace.

A voice came over the public address system at the airport in Atlanta announcing a one-hour delay in our flight. Moans could be heard over the area of Gate 34. Paul and I were tired. We felt the same disappointment. But we both determined to redeem the time by finding the right person for profitable conversation.

Paul found his opportunity first through a phone call to his sister. In the process of telling her what God had been showing him about the Middle East and the end of human government, a young man sat listening with great interest. "Excuse me," the young man said to Paul as soon as he hung up, "But I've never heard what you were talking about. Would you mind explaining more of this subject to me?"

While Paul readily complied, I turned to a businessman sitting to my left. Within a few minutes, I managed to steer the conversation to the subject of this chapter. "It all sounds good, but where is the proof? How can you say Jesus is the true Governor of the world?" he reasoned. "Why not the god of the Hindus, or the Muslims, or Buddhists?"

In recent years, ease of travel and international trade have mixed cultures more thoroughly than any previous generation found possible. There have always been a few select men and women who have traveled the far corners of the earth, but today it is common for some of the masses to do so.

Boston is a multi-cultured, multi-religious city. There are large communities of numerous nationalities. At our center alone, at least seven different languages are spoken at any given meeting.

With this mixing of the masses, there has been an increased awareness of the various world religions. One cannot assume that all Americans know who Jesus is. In the next few pages I am going to list several reasons why it is wise to believe that Jesus alone is the rightful heir and ruler of the nations of this earth.

First Proof: The Pre-Existence of Christ

When a person is going to run for the office of President of the United States, the existing government leaders, the press and the public take a high-powered microscope and begin a thorough investigation of the candidate's credentials. Yet, when it comes to a legal representative for the universal government of God, a man with a good personality, or unique-sounding philosophy can come by and we follow him like a Pied Piper.

For a moment, let us stop and take a look at the claims of Christ, and see how He measures up to the qualifications required of divinity. To do so, it will be necessary for us to go back and consider His early days, prior to Bethlehem. Christ lived before His birth in Israel.

The apostle John, who knew Jesus personally, writes:

> In the beginning was the Word, and the Word was with God, and the Word was God....And the Word was made flesh, and dwelt among us (and we beheld his glory, the glory as of the only begotten of the Father,) full of grace and truth. (John 1:1-14)

In other words, Christ was with Father-God in the beginning. Before the earth or the human race was formed, God and His Son existed. At the appointed time, Christ, the Word, was made flesh, that is, He was born on earth in a human body. He was a man, yet He was God.

Second Proof: He Created the World

Look at what the apostle Paul writes concerning Christ during those days when He preexisted with God.

127

> He is the image of the invisible God, the firstborn over all creation. For by him all things were created: things in heaven and on earth, visible and invisible, whether thrones or powers or rulers or authorities; all things were created by him and for him. (Colossians 1:15-17, NIV)

Stop for a minute. Allow this statement to surface into your consciousness. Christ Jesus preexisted with God from eternity. He created everything that exists in the universe, including the realm of the Spirit. All things were, in fact, created by Him and for Him.

If we will ever appreciate the power and prestige of Christ, we must know Him for who He is. If He is only a babe in a manger, or a broken man on a cross, you will never see Him as the all-powerful Creator He is. Everything from the tiny atom to limitless space, from angelic armies to the human race, all things were created by Christ, the Son of God. "For God was pleased to have all his fullness dwell in him..." (Colossians 1:19, NIV).

How much did God invest in His Son? All of God's plans and power were entrusted to Jesus from the beginning. This means that no additional revelation nor future authority was ever given to any other so-called "great religious leader."

All the gods of men are mere flesh and blood. Their parents were but mortals. The true God had only one Son from the beginning, and God's commission to create the universe was given to Christ.

Therefore, Jesus is distinguished from all other religious leaders by virtue of the fact that He lived with God from the beginning and was assigned the responsibility of creating the world.

Third Proof: He Controls the Universe

A third reason why it is wise to believe in Christ as legal ruler of this earth is found in Hebrews 1:3. Here again we find the apostle Paul telling us that Jesus is continually "upholding all things by the word of his power."

Christ created all things, but He has always had the responsibility of holding creation together. When the human race began to fall apart as a result of sin, it was Jesus who sacrificed himself to retain humanity under God's canopy of grace. If we go back to Hebrews 1:3 to finish the verse, we will find Jesus "upholding all things by the word of his power, when he had by himself purged our sins, sat down on the right hand of the Majesty on high."

Jesus did the job alone. No great thinkers, secluded saints, or ecclesiastical statesmen assisted in the plan of salvation. Jesus was the warrior who faced Satan and took from him the keys to death and hell. By himself He sits at the right hand of God the Father.

- Christ was with God from the beginning of eternity.
- He created the universe.
- He controls the universe.

Fourth Proof: He Ministered in the New Testament

Christ ministered to Israel throughout the period of the Old Testament. Most theologians agree that "the Angel of the Lord" in the Old Testament was actually Christ.

One example of this is found in Judges 13:18, where the angel of the Lord appeared to Samson's parents. When they inquired of His name, the angel replied, "Why askest thou thus after my name, seeing it is secret?"

The word "secret" is from the same Hebrew root found in Isaiah 9:6, where it is translated as *wonderful.* "For unto us a child is born, unto us a son is given, and the government shall be upon his shoulder. And his name shall be called Wonderful..." (Isaiah 9:6).

Isaiah was referring to Jesus when he used the name "Wonderful." In all probability, Samson's parents talked with Christ as "the angel of the Lord." Abraham was visited more than once by the Angel of the Lord. There was a pagan girl named Hagar who received His ministry when she and her son were dying of thirst. Christ was the Cloud, the Pillar of Fire, the Manna and the Rock that provided water for Israel during their years of wandering on the way to Canaan. The apostle Paul, a Hebrew scholar, describes it in First Corinthians 10:1-4:

> Moreover, brethren, I would not that ye should be ignorant, how that all our fathers were under the cloud, and all passed through the sea; And were all baptized unto Moses in the cloud and in the sea; And did all eat the same spiritual meat; And did all drink the same spiritual drink: for they drank of that spiritual Rock that followed them: and that Rock was Christ.

It is false to say that some of the major world religions, such as Confucianism, Shintoism, Buddhism, Hinduism, and Baha'i, are older than Christianity. Christ-followers began with the creation of the human race. Christ has been working with people since the day the Father commissioned Him to form their frail bodies. His incarnation, the birth of Jesus, was simply the last and final stage of Christ's ministry on this earth, before He took His eternal place at the Father's right hand as heir of the universe.

Fifth Proof: His Birth Was Supernatural

- Christ was with God from the beginning.
- He created the world.
- He controls the world.
- He ministered in the Old Testament period.

Next in the line of proof of Jesus' legal right to preside over the governments of this world is the fact of His supernatural birth. Jesus has both natural and supernatural claims to planet earth. No other religious leader can even compare by legal rights to His inherent superiority.

Doubt is ignorance. How foolish the reasonings of man have been down through the ages. How totally bereft of wisdom we have become in our day.

For centuries, so-called great intellects have debated the possibility of the Virgin Birth of Jesus. Many people wonder how any thinking person could actually believe in a virgin conceiving an embryo without sexual intercourse. Such faith seemed naive to those looking through the insufficient eye of logic.

How indeed? Yet this past week on a television documentary, Paul and I watched biological scientists take an animal embryo of one species and plant it into the womb of a different animal. We watched an ordinary brown mare give birth to a zebra-horse with which she had nothing to do, except for carrying it in her womb. According to this transplant method, an elephant could carry and give birth to a hippopotamus, or a dog could carry a kitten. Biologists say this is one way of preserving endangered species.

While I do not wish to comment on the possible negatives of this transplant method, the point is well taken. If a group of mere mortals can plant a fetus into

the womb of an animal and succeed in bringing that
fetus to full-term delivery, surely the great God of all
life could place a living embryo into the womb
of a virgin girl, so that His Son would be born on
this planet.

Why God Sent Christ in Human Form

God did, in fact, send His eternal Son in human form
to represent Him on this earth. He is the one God chose
to enforce the laws of His kingdom and cleanse the earth
of sin and death. He is the one man who is capable of
giving the world an accurate account of the God who sent
Him. And it all makes complete sense when you realize
that you would have done the same if you were God.

Let me ask you, if you needed someone to accurately
describe what you are like, or to carry out your wishes,
would you select a member of your family or would you
ask a neighbor down the street to represent you?

God chose Christ, His Son, to represent Him on this
earth, as Christ alone knows Him best. "No man hath seen
God at any time; the only begotten Son, which is in the
bosom of the Father, he has declared him" (John 1:18).

Even if a human being wanted to be a perfect
representative of the eternal God, he could not do so.
Because of sin, a perfect example would be impossible.
Only perfection can present a true picture of perfection.
Therefore, God planted a sinless embryo into the body
of a virgin. She carried the embryo to development and
Jesus was born with no connection to sinful flesh. And
although he was limited to flesh, perfect flesh was able
to live as a perfect representation of the holy God.

Sixth Proof: He Fulfilled Prophecy

Christ Jesus was a perfect representative of the holy God. He also fulfilled prophecy. "Therefore the Lord himself shall give you a sign; Behold, a virgin shall conceive, and bear a son, and shall call his name Immanuel" (Isaiah 7:14). Stop for a minute. Ask yourself this question: What religious leader has claimed supernatural birth? Does any one of them even pretend to have been parented by persons other than mortal beings? We know the birthplaces and parents of many of the so-called greats. We know from their own journals when they began their religious pilgrimages. Today's pseudo-saviors are clearly identifiable by nationality.

Yet, in Micah 5:2, the prophet said,

> But you, Bethlehem, Ephrathah, though you are little among the thousands of Judah, yet out of you shall come forth to Me the One to be Ruler in Israel; whose goings forth are from of old, from everlasting. (NKJV)

Who was born in Bethlehem? Whose "goings forth" have been from eternity? Jesus Christ. A recent investigation into Scientology here in the United States revealed their leader as a man who lived in seclusion until his death—in order that he might finish developing his philosophy.

When Jesus came on the scene, He did not spend time developing an ideology, but He preached with great authority about a kingdom whose plan was established from the foundations of the world. He ratified that plan by His own shed blood, in total harmony with all the requirements of God's man—according to prophecy.

God sent His Son into the world to perfectly represent himself. He sent Him to guarantee the covenant He made with the house of Israel. The prophets foretold it.

Seventh Proof: He Guarantees God's Covenant with the Royal House of David

Of all the countless reasons we find to believe in Jesus, one of the most exciting proofs of His absolute right to reign on this earth is the fact that only Jesus guarantees God's covenant with the royal house of King David of Israel.

One day Nathan, a prophet in Israel, went to King David and prophesied saying:

> Now therefore, thus shall you say to My servant David, "Thus says the Lord of hosts" I took you from the sheepfold, from following the sheep, to be ruler over My people, over Israel...And your house and your kingdom shall be established forever before you. Your throne shall be established forever.... (2 Samuel 7:8-17, NKJV)

David was a mortal man who died. His son, Solomon, reigned in his place. Eventually their kingdom disappeared. Yet, God promised David that His kingdom "would be established forever." Just how did God plan to keep such a promise?

Listen to what the angel told Mary, when he announced her conception of the Son of God:

And behold, you will conceive in your womb, and bring forth a Son, and shall call His name JESUS. He will be great, and will be called the Son of the Highest: and the Lord God will give Him the throne of His father David: and He will reign over the house of Jacob forever; and of His kingdom there will be no end. (Luke 1:31-33, NKJV)

How exciting! Watch how this unfolds. King David had two sons: Nathan and Solomon. Nathan became the progenitor of Mary's family line; Solomon became the progenitor of Joseph's lineage.

Jesus was born of Mary, who was married to Joseph. Both his natural mother and legal father were of the royal lineage of King David. On both sides of his natural heritage, Jesus has legal right to assume the throne of Israel during the thousand years of peace coming to that nation— and all the earth—called the Millennium.

Jesus is royalty from the bloodline of the royal family who has an eternal covenant with God. This is where He gained His title as King.

Eighth Proof: He Is Qualified to Remove Sins

The whole human race qualifies to talk about sin, but statistics show us that we have yet to come up with a remedy for it. We create laws, and simultaneously, we seek to legalize our violations. No system yet has dealt successfully with moral and spiritual violations. Only Jesus qualified to remove the guilt and penalty of sin from us. Only He had the eternal understanding and authority to break the power of sin by confronting the author of sin who is Satan.

Sin and right conduct are merely the results of two great kingdom systems in mortal combat. Jesus represents

the superior kingdom. Through His death, He was able
to ratify a legal claim to the souls of all who would turn
to God through Jesus' provision.

> For it is not possible that the blood of bulls and
> goats could take away sins....We have been sanctified
> through the offering of the body of Jesus Christ once
> for all...But this Man, after He had offered one
> sacrifice for sins forever, sat down at the right hand
> of God. (Hebrews 10:4-12, NKJV)

The blood of bulls and goats represents all human
effort to become guiltless. It covers the pagan rituals of
self-flagellation, and all Christian rituals of ceremony and
tradition. But nothing on earth, except the shed blood of
Jesus, can cancel the debt of guilt and cleanse our lives
from the consequences of sin.

During one of our countless searches for a building
to purchase for our church, we found a good prospect
being occupied by a group who believed in the value of
all religions. They viewed Jesus as just one good leader
among many. Only fourteen people remained in that
particular assembly and each member was well over sixty
years of age. During the conversation, Paul made
reference to the Christian Church, which prompted the
spry, little woman in charge, to respond, "I was born in
this assembly; I will die in it!"

But being born into a religious assembly will not save
that woman from eternal separation from God. She is
guilty of sin. And until her sin is removed, death has a
legal claim to her soul. This is the reason the Son of God
came to earth—to remove the penalty of sin through faith
in Jesus and to give life to all who will believe.

In Summary

Let us review only a small portion of the countless evidence we could offer for believing that Jesus is the one and only person God has chosen to rule the nations of this earth. Let us draw a clear picture of His divine royalty as the Son of God, as well as His natural nobility through the lineage of King David. Let us compare His qualifications with those of other so-called great religious leaders. Let us respond to that element of faith within our hearts that recognizes the truth when we hear it.

- Christ Jesus is the Son of God who preexisted
- He controls the universe.
- Christ ministered in the Old Testament.
- His birth was supernatural.
- He fulfilled prophecy.
- He guarantees God's covenant with the royal house of David.
- He is qualified to remove the sins of the world.

Until Jesus returns to rule this earth, we can expect many nations to continue parading their false gods as heralds of truth. In the face of great revival there will also be a great departure from biblical faith. But one day Jesus will return, and then it will all make so much sense that men are going to grind their teeth at their blindness. The day the Son of God declares His authority on our planet, there will be a mass closing of every major institution on the earth. The financial districts will abandon their offices of greed in shame. All the great libraries, museums, universities, and tourist temple sites will rush to bolt their doors.

The ignorance of man's words.
The ignorance of man's art.
The ignorance of man's spirit.

All will be suddenly exposed and become painfully useless.

Libraries will be allowed to reopen only after they have been thoroughly restocked with volumes of truth and wisdom. There will not be one book exalting avowed atheists whose works supposedly changed the course of history. We will then understand that no man can slow down, much less alter, the course God has established for His universe.

When Jesus returns to earth, the museums of fine arts will undergo drastic house-cleaning. All of Picasso's paintings will be put on sale for the price of hauling them away, along with every other expression of distortion and confusion. His and other similar "paint-jobs" by lives out of focus will be deftly whisked through the back door for the daily garbage pick-up service. These trucks will not be allowed to move quickly, however, as there will be long lines of traffic at the entrance to the local incinerators, waiting to dump all the plastic tapes of the world's obscene rock artists. And not one person will run to congress yelling, "Censorship!"

International tourism will, at this time, undergo a temporary upheaval as the pagan temple sites, plus all institutions of doubt, are being bulldozed and cleared away as parking spaces for the new houses of honor to Messiah. And then one of the clever agencies will suddenly remember God's prophecy concerning all those people who will want to view the valley where Jesus defeated Gog's army, and color brochures will start rolling off the presses!

Then, standing in the glorious presence of the true King and Governor of nations, all human logic will begin to creep back obediently into place, and proof will be as common as grass. Jesus will then assume the throne of world government for 1,000 years of planet-wide restoration. It will be called the Kingdom Age, or as John wrote in Revelation 20, the Millennium.

13

A Signal From Russia

Several of today's eschatologists see Russia as a key figure in the events of the last days. Certainly Russia is equipped to play an important role. Its large Islamic population and unique history of oppression qualifies Russia to be one of the key players in the decisions regarding the Middle East. In this chapter I want us to take a brief trip into Russian history. Perhaps there, more than in any other industrialized country, we can get a picture of the movement of dominating principalities and powers as they seek to control the people of the world. Having traveled in the old Eastern Bloc for twenty years, I had almost forgotten the stern, blank stares on the faces of the people in that part of the world. Even after some years of relative freedom from oppressive communist domination, during a recent visit I was struck by the fact that no one in public yet smiles or favorably responds outwardly. The more I learn about Russian history, the more I understand why this is true. Oppression has been their way of life for at least 1,000 years! Enslaved by a millennium of oppression, it has rightly been called "a country of slaves, a country of masters."

By the middle of the nineteenth century, parliamentary democracies or constitutional monarchies had been established throughout most of Europe. Yet in Russia, peasants remained under the iron fists of autocratic rulers. Even the aristocrat was not safe. It was said that living close to the czar was like "walking on the rim of a volcano" (Mikhail Iroshnikov, *Sunset of the Romanov Dynasty*, Terra Publishing Centre, Moscow, 1992, p. 10).

The *system* of government under the czars in pre-communist Russia was a triad: "orthodoxy, autocracy [unlimited power of the monarchy] and *narodnost* [intense nationalism]." This was the triune power system that energized "Holy Russia" for hundreds of years. It was a system that, "supported both the church and the throne, and to uproot it [was] impossible" (Ibid, p. 14). Or so it was believed.

When the revolutions began in 1825 and advanced to the Bolshevik Revolution and the overthrow of Czar Nicholas II in 1917, communism took over with the promise of equality. After years of communist impoverishment and the fall of the Berlin Wall in 1989, the doors to religion flew open and for the first time in centuries there seemed to be hope.

In 1993, however, the old oppression raised its ugly head once again through the Orthodox Church and some Russian nationals who drafted a proposal that would greatly paralyze missionary work there. According to an article in *The Wall Street Journal*, the religious revival that began after the break up of the Soviet Union soon began to look like a threat to the dominance of the Russian Orthodox Church, "a centuries-old institution that doesn't want to miss the chance to reclaim its once-powerful role" (Gerald F. Seib, *The Wall Street Journal*, March 17, 1993, p. A10, col. 3), and they have begun to throw up roadblocks ever since.

What does it all mean? The Bible tells us clearly that, "We do not wrestle against flesh and blood, but against principalities, against powers, against the rulers of the darkness of this age, against spiritual hosts of wickedness in the heavenly places" (Ephesians 6:12, NKJV).

Ruling princes in the second heavens (fallen angels in Satan's kingdom) work through governments and religious systems on this earth to enslave the souls of men. Satan is called the one who "didst weaken [prostrate, overthrow] the nations" (Isaiah 14:12). Revolutions, monarchies, or religious institutions that oppress people are knowingly or unknowingly pawns for the powers of Satan.

Does this mean that all leaders within a government and all members of religious hierarchies are evil? No. God has put both civil and religious governments on the earth. Men need to be governed. Human nature must be restrained or social chaos will prevail. That is the problem in America today. Children have been turned loose by parents who have themselves abandoned all moral and spiritual restraints. Statistically, the result is that America has become twice as violent as any other western nation. I walked off a plane at Heathrow Airport in London, and staring me in the face was a magazine with a large headline, "America the Violent." No longer are we called "America the Beautiful," but the world sees us as a totally unrestrained society.

Man and Government

From the Garden of Eden, God made it clear that man needs government. Even righteous Adam had a ceiling over his behavior. Rebelling against government is what brought about the fall of the human race. Government is ordained of God. Yet, government is the one thing man resists. Rebellion against authority is the seedbed for all our present evils. As a result of Adam's rebellion against God's kingdom, he joined forces with the "arch-rebel," Satan. Since that time, ungodly power permeates any form of government possible—civil or religious. Does this mean that all rulers and church officials are Satan's emissaries? No, it means that any ruler or church official who does not know, understand, and adhere to the Word of God is subject to be used by Satan. Government is ordained of God, but lust for power sometimes causes men to be used by Satan.

Ruthless and Righteous

For 300 years, the Romanov family ruled Russia. In reading the life of the last czar of Russia, one is immediately struck by a paradox that followed Nicholas from unbelievable wealth and Christian decency to the semi-basement of a home in Siberia, where he and his entire family were executed by a nation in revolt against him.

Czar Nicholas and his wife, Alexandra, were, from all accounts of their personal diaries and public behavior, a genuinely God-fearing couple. Alexandra's Protestant influence was brought into the royal family's Orthodoxy, and together they pursued a truly spiritual life.

Nicholas wrote to his mother about the Easter celebration of 1900, "I never knew that I was capable of reaching such heights of spiritual rapture as those which the present Lent has revealed to me. My present feeling is much stronger than the one I had in 1896, which is quite natural. Now I am so calm and happy, and everything here inspires to prayer and brings conciliation to the soul" (Ibid, p. 142).

As for the Empress Alexandra, it is written, "Her very first contributions to Nicholas' diary show that she was literally crammed full of religions homilies and maxims, constantly aware of her dependence on divine providence, and even conducted by it in her daily life" (Ibid, p. 141).

Yet, history shows this couple to have been seemingly oblivious to the decline of autocratic monarchies such as theirs. They appeared to be blind to the economic changes taking place in the rest of the world—and the groundswell of dissatisfaction among their own pathetic peasantry. Indifference to abuse of the poor was a feature of Nicholas's reign which had been passed down to him from centuries of serfdom.

Serfs were people who were owned by the wealthy. They could buy no property or ever hope for anything but lifelong poverty. Serfs were often given as gifts by their master. They could be traded or sold as a man traded or sold his animals. Starvations, drownings, exiles to Siberia, beatings, Jewish massacres, beastly retaliations against any protest, war machines—this constituted the life of the Russian serf. Although serfdom was legally done away with by Nicholas's grandfather, Alexander II, this decent, family-loving, God-fearing man never seemed to recognize his own responsibility to help bring about real change for the people. Shortly before his execution by the revolutionaries, Nicholas had his daughter send the following prophetic pronouncement of what lay just ahead for his people

> Father asks you to tell all those who remain loyal to him, and those with whom they might have influence, not to take revenge for him, because he has forgiven everyone and prays for everyone, and to remember that the evil that is now in the world will be stronger yet, but that it is not evil which overcomes evil, but only love. (Ibid, p. 34)

How is it that a person can be both ruthless and righteous? How can a government be both civil and barbaric, as America now is, passing out prophylactics and killing one and one-half million babies each year before they have even had a chance to cry? Conscientious on the one hand, but practicing unconscionable acts on the other, how can we avoid the fate that befell Czar Nicholas because he failed to discern his day?

There is only one way to avoid being washed away with the confusion of distorted standards in any generation, and that is by taking heed to the Word of God. Standards for human behavior cannot be decided by human beings—be they aristocrats or peasants. The czars murdered the peasants, the peasants murdered the czars and anyone else with any degree of education and influence. The communist revolution ultimately murdered more ordinary people than royal family members. It murdered more educators than palace guards. There must be a higher standard than human ideologies if we hope to avoid increasing bloodshed. America and the Western World cannot rest on a vague "save the animals" compassion and hope to restore civil obedience. We must develop a conscience that is more "bone-scraping" than one that holds only to compassion for the environment if we want to bring violence to human beings under control.

Unlimited Blessing - Deteriorating Curse

The Garden of Eden had the potential for unlimited blessing or devastating curse. Adam chose the curse. By rejecting the Word of God, he brought a 6,000-year-long curse on society that has multiplied into our present state of violence. The wisdom of God is the only salvation for the human race. It is accountability to God's Word that will keep human nature in check at every level of society. *The Word of God alone has the power to challenge the "principalities and powers" that manipulate and operate through Word-starved religious systems and human governments.* The attempt to stop missionary work in Russia or any part of the world is effort energized by "ancient principalities" that have enslaved and weakened the nations throughout history. What the world needs in this hour is not a revival of liturgy and ceremony, but a revival of Spirit-empowered truth.

Orthodoxy needs this revival so that it ceases to be a pawn for the powers of darkness. Catholicism needs this revival so that it arms its people with a personal knowledge of God's Word above Church ritual and tradition. Materialistic Protestant churches in America and other western nations need this revival so that they will stop lulling the people into the psychology of self-realization and religious achievement. "Truth has fallen into the streets," as the prophet predicted. It is being trampled by an unrestrained generation rapidly becoming serfs to money *hungry people in the world and spiritually impaired clergy in the pulpits.*

147

How can we know what is truth? We cannot without a frame of reference. Only by using the Word of God as our standard can we see clearly what course of action to take. It is unpopular to say so, but churchgoers need to take a close look at the pulpits of the churches they attend. The character of the person standing in the pulpit should reflect a life under control. A pastor recently accused of adultery responded, "Look, I'm not perfect. I'm just as human as you are." Any pastor who has lost control of his life forfeits his place in the pulpit until he proves a genuine repentance. God has placed ministers as examples to the Church. Paul wrote, "Our gospel came not unto you in word only, but also in power, and in the Holy Ghost, and in much assurance; as you know what manner of men we were among you for your sake" (1 Thessalonians 1:5).

People need to look at the character of the persons occupying the pulpits, and they need to listen to what is being said. The Bible says, "Where the spirit of the Lord is there is liberty." Any person, church, or religious system that attempts to keep people ignorant of the Bible and the present moves of the Holy Spirit is oppressive and not operating by the Spirit of God. The primary purpose of every priest or pastor is to instruct people in the Word of God and to lead them to seek God for present truth on a personal basis. A relationship with God is a personal transaction, not a group impartation. "Watching over the sheep" does not include legally enforcing a specific tradition or liturgy on the people. The pulpit was not established for dictators, but rather for instructors to impart God's Word and His will for today.

Just listening to the conversation of ordinary people as we travel today in the former Soviet Union, I realize why communism never took hold in America the way a few "vacant lots" in education and the media wanted. A people well-versed in the Scriptures has preserved America from political suicide. Strong families, the right to bear arms, the right to own property, accountability to the standards of God's Word, recognizing error when we hear it, moral decency—this is what has kept the free world from becoming serfs to power-hungry, career-mad Frankensteins. But I question if that same wisdom exists today in most circles.

A Call to Alarm

A few years ago I read a magnificent work entitled *The Sunset of the Romanov Dynasty* by Mikhail Iroshnikov. About midway through the book, I began to see that it was actually a preview of "The Sunset of the World System." The reign of the famous Czar Nicholas II, opens with his riding into the Moscow Kremlin on a white horse surrounded by a degree of splendor most of us only dream about. One reporter wrote of that event,

> There was a mass of spectators looking out of every window: here were the gleaming uniforms of British admirals, and Spaniards and Japanese, and Chinese, and beautiful French cavalry officers in gleaming, gilded helmets in the ancient Greek style with horsetails streaming out behind. The whole of the long balcony was taken up by a great number of extremely elegant society ladies in magnificent white costumes and hats.... At half past two the bells of all the churches in Moscow.... announced the fact that the parade had begun.... They drove the senators past in golden carriages.... The rulers of the Asian people pranced past.... All in robes embroidered with golden wonderful race horses.... The soldiers presented arms,

149

> the music struck up and the young Czar appeared on
> a white Arab horse.... At ten in the evening the
> illuminations were turned on. A magical fairy tale
> began, a waking dream. People walked as
> if spellbound among glowing precious
> stones...admiring the exotic sight. (Ibid, pp. 26-27)

That was the opening of Czar Nicholas's life. It ended sadly with the Czar sitting on a stump in Siberia, his face deeply lined, his hands hanging in a lifeless fold, abandoned by everyone and awaiting his execution.

How could it be that a Czar with a spiritually sensitive heart did so little to change the circumstances of his world? The answer is simple. He was blind to reality! His spirituality remained uneducated by the Spirit and the Word. He never got the bigger view of life. His own comfortable world, his preconditioned view of life passed down through his tradition told him that all was well, normal, decent. He lived a "waking dream...spellbound...among exotic sights." And his three-hundred-year-old dynasty fell into oblivion in only three short days.

And so it has been with man in every generation. Whether blinded by wealth or poverty, the focus of life has been largely our own personal world of survival and success. What is more, it has been a Gentile vision which misses the plan of God altogether and feeds into the endless struggles nations have continued to reenact for 6,000 years. From generation to generation, the script has been the same—only the actors have changed. Egypt, Assyria, Babylon, Medo-persia, Greece, Rome, Spain, Great Britain, Germany, Russia, the United States. We have been handed the same script; we have memorized the same lines, fought the same wars; and we are no closer to a peaceful resolution to the human plight than when we began.

A Different Script

Among the thousands of nations that have existed, only one nation has been handed a different script to read and a different role to play. That nation is Israel. The disciples once came to Jesus with a question, "...Lord, will You at this time restore the kingdom to Israel?" (Acts 1:6, NKJV). Jesus' response has been begging to be understood for 2,000 years. "It is not for you to know times or seasons which the Father has put in His own authority" (Acts 1:7, NKJV).

In other words, "Yes, the kingdom would be restored in Israel when God is ready." But why? Why should this tiny nation, instead of a more advanced, prestigious empire, experience royal resurrection?

Get hold of the answer to this question and you will advance light-years in understanding what lies ahead. Israel will have its kingdom restored and exalted above all other kingdoms because *Israel is the only nation that never had a natural kingdom.* From its inception, Israel's kingdom was a divine government, birthed and directed by God himself.

In David, God established the beginning stages of the Kingdom of Heaven on earth. David's was the "seed-throne" that will one day become the throne of Christ during the Millennial Kingdom Age. Gabriel announced it so:

> Now in the sixth month the angel Gabriel was sent by God to a city of Galilee named Nazareth, to a virgin betrothed to a man whose name was Joseph,

151

of the house of David. The virgin's name was Mary.
...Then the angel said to her, "Do not be afraid, Mary,
for you have found favor with God. And behold, you
will conceive in your womb and bring forth a Son, and
shall call His name JESUS. He will be great, and will
be called the Son of the Highest; and the Lord God
will give Him the throne of His father David." (Luke
1:26, 30-32, NKJV)

Through King David, God created an opening whereby
He would reenter the political scene once again, and
superimpose His government over every other government
begun in Adamic rebellion.

We like to say that western thinking was birthed by
Aristotle. Much of what we think in math, science, religion,
and culture was shaped by this impressive thinker. But
pagan ideology began with Adam. Adam was the first
human being to think apart from and in contradiction to
God. Every other pagan thought or system of thought was
birthed out of him.

Every government besides Israel's has had a human
origin. Some governments were originally based on godly
principles, such as the United States of America. Yet the
government itself was not divine, as is obvious by its
decay. There is only one divine government. It originates
in the Kingdom of Heaven. That is the government which
is coming down to earth and will flow out of the nation of
Israel, from the ancient throne of David. In view of his
monumental mistakes, have you ever wondered why God
used David and referred to him as "a man after my own
heart"? It was because David, in spite of his flaws, desired
and pursued the establishment of the Kingdom of God on
this earth. Jesus said, "Seek first the Kingdom." That is,
seek the bringing in of God's divine government to
earth. It is the only government that will work on a
long-term basis.

Ancient Israel had many kings. Most were carnal and blind to the fact that they were actually seated on a divine, eternal throne in proxy of the Adonai, Messiah himself. Israel had many high priests—some good, some carnal—who watched over the souls of God's people in the stead of the great High Priest. Israel had three beautiful temples built by Solomon, Zerubbabel, and Herod. In 70 A.D., God removed all human kings and high priests from Messiah's earthly throne place. At this moment in history, Messiah's earthly throne is empty and there is no temple among us. God has allowed this so that Satan's throne might come to fruition. The antichrist is next on the agenda. He will precede the coming of Christ and His kingdom only by a few months. It will be man's last attempt to govern himself apart from God.

Christ is destined to take the burden of the nations upon His shoulders. He will take the worship of the people upon His heart as the Great High Priest.

> Even he shall build the temple of the Lord; and he shall bear the glory, and shall sit and rule upon his throne; and he shall be a priest upon his throne: and the counsel of peace shall be between them both [the offices of both priest and king]. (Zechariah 6:13)

In clear, unmistakable language, history leads to an appointed end.

Now I ask you a question which God recently proposed to me: *"Do you love God?"* It is an age-old question to which Simon Peter answered, "Yes, Lord, you know I love you."

But then God came back with a stinging question that is still burning in my soul today, *"Do you also love my plans, as you love me?"*

It is not enough to say, "I believe in God," or even to say "I love Him." If our eyes will be open to the reality of what is taking place in our day, we must also love God's plans—God's plans for our life personally, God's plans for our world, God's plans for the Church called by His name.

Since 1948, the nation of Israel has been in a national revival. Since 1990, the nation of the Church has been in an international revival. It is the day to rise up and complete the commission given to us by the Lord Jesus—Yeshua—"Go and make disciples of all nations." The Spirit of God is being poured out afresh for that purpose. It's a call to the Church to arise!

14

The Last Hour

A sense of the end of all things has dogged man in every generation; conversely, the possibility of new beginnings has always goaded him forward. Man usually senses the truth long before he discovers the facts to back it up.

Orville and Wilbur Wright were not sitting in a physics class studying the science of aviation when they decided to build a vehicle that would fit their dream. They first sensed a desire to fly. Birds could fly; a piece of paper thrown up in the air could fly for a short distance. Why not man? The laws were there all the time. No doubt the facts were painfully obvious once the mystery began to unravel. But the skies remained empty of airplanes until the sense of such a possibility uncovered the facts.

The fact is that the end of human existence, as we know it, is certain. The government of politics, religion, and social behavior, as we know it, is coming to an end. Man's way of life is dying. Life itself will not come to an end, but new beginnings are destined to emerge out of the ruins of the present system.

A sense of the end and a sense of new beginnings are equally valid. Both principles have been in operation since sin entered creation. From the moment man took over the destiny of his own life he has been dying. At the same time, from the moment he began to respond to a sense of faith tugging at him, he has begun to live again.

The great mystery of humanity is that birth is taking place on the mound of the grave, and that one day death is destined to be swallowed up by life. What we need, without sorrow or regret, is to identify death and let it die. At the same time, we need to identify life and cooperate fully with its operation in our generation.

The world has always had a poor record of identifying death at work in its ungodly system. Similarly, the Church has always had a poor record of identifying life at work in its godly system. Human nature feels uncomfortable with change. Although everything about us is in a continual state of motion, we prefer the holding pattern to landing and facing the challenge. Yet time moves forward and we continue to find ourselves caught up in events we rarely understand.

It is to be expected that the world should not understand the life-and-death struggle going on around people. I picked up a magazine to read its headline announcement of a young Hollywood star who was dying with AIDS. "I just don't understand," he said. "How could it happen to me when I have so much left to give?"

But the Church can lay claim to no such excuse. We can and should—indeed, we must—come to understand what is happening in our world if we will ever flow with what God is doing in our generation. We must acknowledge that the events prophesied about for thousands of years will occur, and as they occur, changes will take place. According to the Scriptures, the Church will receive greater and greater enlightenment as the last hour draws near. New understanding will appear increasingly among God's people.

Changes in government, changes in social behavior, and changes in the Church are all foretold. Yet only those people who are open to new understanding will cooperate with the "death of the world system" and the "birth of divine authority" that is coming in full measure to this spinning little planet.

We are the last generations. This is the end time. Human history is coming to a close. Almost 2,000 years ago, the apostle John wrote, "Little children, it is the last time: and as ye have heard that antichrist shall come, even now are there many antichrists; whereby we know that it is the last time" (1 John 2:18).

The apostle Peter wrote: "...the end of all things is at hand..." (1 Peter 4:7).

The Apostle Paul wrote of Jesus, "...but now once in the end of the world hath he appeared to put away sin by the sacrifice of himself" (Hebrews 9:26).

The *birth* of Jesus marked the *beginning of the end* of all things as we know them. The *return* of Jesus to earth will mark the *end of the end*.

Compared to the universe, humanity is young; but because of sin it has aged quickly. Therefore, God has not allowed a long season for sin to rob and kill His creation. John said clearly it is the "last hour."

Pastor Paul, my husband, was called to the bedside of a dying young man. As the pastor's style goes, he came straight to the point. The young man's condition was AIDS. After introducing himself, by way of the person who had asked him to make the call, Paul declared, "I'm here to talk to you about eternal life in the Kingdom of God."

"Nonsense," the man responded.

"God sent His Son to earth to die for your sins," Paul continued. "Through the shed blood of Jesus you can have eternal life."

"I'm not interested in a pagan religion that has blood sacrifices," the young man responded. "I serve a god of love."

"Your god couldn't be too loving," Paul pleaded. "Look where he has brought you!"

After a few more minutes of trying to reason with him, sadly Paul left the young man in his darkness. Because a person has reached the end does not mean he understands the end.

And so it goes with humanity. The "last hour" will not be recognized by the majority of people. Degeneration is never obvious to those involved in the process—surprisingly, neither is spiritual revival. Yet the Bible says these two conditions will develop into full maturity during the closing minutes of the "last hour"—*dramatic degeneration in the world and revival in the true Church.*

This dramatic degeneration will occur in government, social behavior, and all other human institutions. This dramatic degeneration, along with dramatic spiritual revival, is a signal of the "last hour." Governments, society, and the Church—all three—will be approaching the end of the runway. Two will crash, one will become airborne, and only those who are wise will understand what is happening.

Governments and Society

In America's mad rush to make sure we have separation of church and state, we have overlooked a hard reality—it is the purpose of government to maintain morality. The very nature and duty of law is to enforce social good. A government with no position of rights and wrongs is not only immoral; it is also worthless.

Listen to God's description of such a government: "You lie and grumble and oppose the good. No one cares about being fair and true. Your lawsuits are based on lies.... Our courts oppose the righteous man; fairness is unknown. Truth falls dead in the streets, and justice is outlawed. Yes, truth is gone, and anyone who tries a better life is soon attacked. The Lord saw all the evil and was displeased to find no steps taken against sin" (Isaiah 59:3-4,14-15, TLB).

Morality is a social law as scientific as gravity. It is the duty of government to uphold morality, to take steps to maintain a standard of moral decency for the common good. Governments that do not fall under the breath of God as He calls out, 'O pleasure-mad kingdom, living at ease, bragging as the greatest in the world—listen to the sentence of my court upon your sins.' You say, 'I alone am God!' You felt secure in all your wickedness. 'No one sees me,' you said. Your wisdom and knowledge have caused you to turn away from me and claim that you yourself are Jehovah. That is why disaster shall overtake you suddenly—so suddenly that you won't know where it comes from. And there will be no atonement to cleanse away your sins" (Isaiah 47:8,10-11, TLB).

This is the fate of governments in the closing hour of human rule over the nations. Intoxicated with pleasure or impressed by their own knowledge, disintegration will consume the nations that presume to have answers apart from God. Decay will grip the very core of civil restraint, and fallen human nature will pour out its evil at every level of society.

The "last hour" of human government will have two distinguishing marks that differentiate it from all preceding governments.

I. God's favor will be removed from man–leaving him to his own limitations.

II. Events will go beyond remedy, policy deadlocks and civil unrest will prevail.

This is the result of apostasy. According to the Scriptures, people in the "last hour" will no longer seek God. Both leaders and citizenry will be gods unto themselves. When this happens, God ceases to retain His hand of protection over them. Isaiah describes it as a day when the leaders abandon the care of the people and chaos prevails. "God has removed his protecting care. You run to the armory for your weapons! ...But all your feverish plans will not avail, for you never ask for help from God..." (Isaiah 22:8, 11, TLB).

After discovering that foreign tourists were being targeted for robbery and murder in America, I watched a man from the State Department discuss the subject in a way that so infuriated me I got out of bed and penned an article, which I faxed the next day to the major newspapers in Boston, New York, and London. Two days later a call from one of London's leading newspapers, *The European*, picked up the article for publication. The following was birthed out of that original thought.

Is America Sick?

In response to the on-going accusations that "America has become a sick society," may I speak for millions of Americans with a resounding, "Yes, the average American is sick!"

We are sick of a sex-soaked, violence-ridden film and entertainment industry that preys on vulnerable people, portraying every base act of human nature twenty-four hours a day in our homes and theaters.

We are sick of the so-called experts spewing out psychological nonsense that excuses every act of personal irresponsibility because of some painful childhood experience. Who hasn't had it tough in this world?

We are sick of young people saying, "I wouldn't be lawless if I had a job." Go to work! Clean up the place where you live. Repair broken items. Cook meals for your mother, who probably is working. Pick up litter on your street. Read a book. Learn a musical instrument. Go to school and make the honor roll.

Yes, **the average American is sick!** We are sick of an educational system that banned the Ten Commandments and instituted sexual emphasis programs, with counseling for abortion and numerous disease-spreading, immoral life-styles that supposedly can be controlled by passing out free condoms.

We are sick of a court system that refuses to process convicted criminals promptly. **We are sick** of a penal system that has lost the will to punish. **We are sick** of mob rule that demands legal action. Freedom of expression does not guarantee court action.

And **we are sick** of an impotent government that has lost the courage to govern. In America's mad rush to ensure separation of church and state, it has overlooked a hard reality—it is the purpose of government to maintain moral standards of behavior. The very nature of law is to enforce social good. A government with no position of rights and wrongs is not only immoral, it is worthless! And **we are sick** of career politicians who stand for nothing but reelection.

We are sick of a money-mad toy industry which produces violence-infested, occult-ridden items that train our children to release themselves to powers they know nothing about—all under the guise of "games."

And **we are sick** of career-hungry, television talk-show hosts who are getting rich off "sleaze" that dignifies indecency and helps to produce moral corrosion. And **we are sick** of vulgar, violent lyrics set to loud, music and accompanied by obnoxious gyrations that together are called concert performances.

The average American is sick of hearing that our youth would be "good" if only they had a "better chance" in life. It takes more than a "chance" to build values and respect for human life into a person.

The rural community where I grew up was so poor only two families owned a vehicle and one telephone existed for everybody. Each family owned a gun cabinet with several guns, yet no one ever shot another human being. Why? Because our whole society taught us that human life is sacred, and that any person who violated this standard would be held personally accountable. "Take away the guns!" is the great cry today, and we could. But overfed, unrestrained violence in the heart will only find other weapons unless we deal with the systems that are feeding into our present bankrupt mind-set.

When man no longer seeks God, and God no longer protects man from his own inherent evil nature, there is no remedy for that generation and social collapse is certain. This is both the desire and the destiny of the last generations. King David prophesied (in Psalm 2) that the Gentiles would one day reach a point where the leaders and people together would agree to throw off all godly restraint from their lives.

What fools the nations are to rage against the Lord! How strange that men should try to outwit God! For a summit conference of the nations has been called to plot against the Lord and his Messiah, Christ the King. Come, let us break His chains, they say, and free ourselves from all this slavery to God.

Freedom from religion is the universal theme of the men of the last hour. They seek a moral license, an individual right to do whatever brings pleasure.

The Church

But Isaiah said, "Look, a righteous King is coming with honest princes" (Isaiah 32:1). [A moral president with moral senators is coming!] "In those days the ungodly, the atheists, will not be heroes! Wealthy cheaters will not be spoken of as generous, outstanding men! Everyone will recognize an evil man when he sees one, and hypocrites will fool no one....The smooth tricks of evil men will be exposed, as will all the lies they use to oppress the poor in the courts" (Isaiah 32:1, 5-7).

Have you noticed how tenderly the cameras rush to exalt the generosity of profane, immoral people? It matters little how personally degenerate a person may live, so long as he makes a financial contribution to society—or runs for public office under the guise of a public servant.

A very competent surgeon in New York attempted to murder his wife. After removing all his cash from the bank, he then faked his own death. When the doctor returned, the reporters went into his local area for comment. Amazingly, almost all the people agreed that he was a wonderful person who should return immediately to his practice. Simply because of his medical skills the people lauded a corrupt individual as a hero.

Fortunately, however, there is another side to the "last hour" generation. Not all men will be deceived in the closing minutes of history. Not all people of the last hour will be stumbling around in the dark. When everything in society is being tested, governments are failing, men are being stripped of power and position, the godly are going to be rewarded. Isaiah said, "...All is well for the godly man. Tell him, "What a reward you are going to get!" (Isaiah 3:10). But what are the godly supposed to be doing in the last hour that will earn this reward? While the evil are spreading chaos and confusion, what is the responsibility of the righteous?

As much as the Church is responsible to maintain the practical responsibilities of daily life, the focus of the last hour is clearly upon the Spirit. The Church has been empowered with the full authority of heaven to proclaim Jesus in the last hour, and there are two ways by which this will be accomplished:

1. Frequent corporate worship and study of the Word.
2. The ministry of the Holy Spirit.

The apostle Paul wrote of this hour.

> ...not forsaking the assembling of yourselves together, as is the manner of some, but exhorting one another, and so much the more as you see the Day approaching (Hebrews 10:25, NKJV).

The true Church will increase in strength as the Day of the Lord draws nearer. According to the Book of Acts a great ministry of the Holy Spirit will be manifested in the local body. Through average church members, both men and women, spiritual dreams, visions, and prophecies will occur in the Church of the "last hour." Along with these abundant revelations, God will also give cosmic signs in the heavens and startling signs through nature. The powers of heaven will literally be in demonstration upon the earth—both Satan's powers and God's.

Could the outpouring of great joy and liberty in worship the Church is presently experiencing be a herald of these signs? Since 1993, our church, the Christian Teaching and Worship Center, on the north shore of Boston, has been experiencing a great visitation of the Holy Spirit. Worship and praise have blossomed into a joy we never dreamed possible. We are shouting, singing, and dancing as David leaped before the Ark. Several members of our congregation and I have written hundreds of beautiful, anointed songs of worship and praise. Many of the songs were written spontaneously during the worship service itself. Relationships have been restored, repentance has abounded, physical healings have occurred, beautiful prophetic utterances from the congregation have flowed like poetry and we have lost all fear of man. Surely it is a foretaste of that end-time outpouring.

The coming of the Holy Spirit to earth at Pentecost was accomplished with great signs and wonders. It marked the beginning of the end. The end of the end will be even more dramatic. The glorious demonstrations of the powers of heaven in mortal combat with the powers of evil will be plain for all to see. The "last hour" is the end of all perishable things and the birth of new and eternal beginnings. The prophet says there has never been such a day before, nor will one follow to equal it.

15

Elijah Is Coming

Enroute to a conference where I was speaking, I was looking down at the billowing clouds when a startling statement darted across my thoughts, "Elijah is coming."

The Church has basically accommodated the belief in the return of the Lord, based on: (1) Israel's long held message of a coming Messiah, and (2) the testimony of two angels who appeared after the Ascension of Jesus. "Who also said, 'Ye men of Galilee, why stand ye gazing up into heaven? This same Jesus, which is taken up from you into heaven, shall so come in like manner as ye have seen Him go into heaven" (Acts 1:11). Many are looking for Jesus to come as He went, but who in our day has given serious thought to the return of Elijah, except observant Jews who pour a cup of wine for the prophet and leave the door ajar for his appearing at Passover?

Taking my Bible and opening it to the very last chapter of the Old Testament, I began to read with anticipation:

Behold, I will send you Elijah the prophet before the coming of the great and dreadful day of the Lord. And he will turn the hearts of the fathers to the children, and the hearts of the children to their fathers, lest I come and strike them with a curse." (Malachi 4:5-6, NKJV)

Jesus is coming again. Before He does, Elijah is coming down to minister on the earth for three-and-a-half years. For those who are disconcerted with the present supernatural phenomena going on in the Church today, I wonder what they would do with the ministry of Elijah, should we be the generation to see the Lord return? This was the question I began to ponder, on my flight to the conference. If we question and debate "holy laughter," what would we say about a man dressed in sackcloth, like the ancient prophets, going about Israel performing miracles. Would we believe the story that he was turning water into blood? Or would we accept that God was telling him to cause droughts and human suffering? Would we believe it, or better still, would we agree with such tactics?

According to Malachi, the wicked systems of wicked men are going to be removed from the earth, beginning with the Second Coming of Messiah. Evil itself will not disappear overnight, but its power base will be cast into Sheol, along with Satan and his followers. The earth itself is not going to be irradiated, however, and this is important to understand if we want to be consistent with both the Old and New Testaments.

In the Old Testament Malachi said:

"For behold, the day is coming, burning like an oven, and all the proud, yes, all who do wickedly will be stubble. And the day which is coming shall burn them up," says the Lord of hosts, "That will leave them neither root nor branch. But to you who fear My name the Sun of Righteousness shall arise with healing in His wings; and you shall go out and grow fat like stall-fed calves." (Malachi 4:1-2, NKJV)

In the New Testament Paul wrote,

And to give you who are troubled rest with us when the Lord Jesus is revealed from heaven with His mighty angels, in flaming fire taking vengeance on those who do not know God, and on those who do not obey the gospel of our Lord Jesus Christ. (2 Thessalonians. 1:7-8, NKJV)

East/West Philosophy

To explain the coming purging of this earth let us go back in history for a minute. The Church has always fluctuated between eastern and western thought, regarding the age to come. Western thought began in Greece where philosophers like Socrates and Plato taught that the universe had both a plan and a purpose. Judaism and Christianity then came along and explained this plan as one God, who created and ordered the universe under specific and dependable laws. To the western mind-set, all creation is valuable and has an eternal plan in God's scheme of things. Jesus said, "The meek shall inherit the earth." But how could they do so if He planned to destroy the earth at His coming?

Eastern thought, on the other hand, has always held to polytheism (the worship of many gods). Philosophically, Eastern thinking believes that only a realm outside this earth is of any value. Therefore, they seek to reach this better world by denying themselves and this present world of matter and material things.

Simply stated, eastern thinking believes this world ultimately has no value because it is not permanent. Therefore, one must meditate and discipline himself to achieve that better world beyond this earth. This is where reincarnation comes in. Eastern religion believes the soul goes through many cycles of birth, death and rebirth, on its way to that other realm.

What does the Bible teach regarding natural creation? What did Malachi mean when he said, "The day cometh that shall burn as an oven?" What is going to burn? Is God going to destroy the earth? When we die will we never see this   world again?

For the answer to those questions, let us begin at the beginning. In Genesis 1, we learn that God created the heavens and the earth and He, "...saw that it was good." Creation is not evil; it is good. However, at some point in the past, an evil system was introduced into creation— first in heaven and then on earth.

The Birth of Evil

Isaiah 14:12-15 describes the birth of evil in heaven through the rebellion of a powerful angel named Lucifer. God purged heaven of Lucifer and one-third of the angels who rebelled with him. Following his eviction, Lucifer (Satan) then turned his attention to the earth, where God had placed a prize- creation called man, modeled in His very own image. Satan, speaking through the serpent, tempted and succeeded in causing God's prize model to rebel against His kingdom authority. Now God's "good creation" had an evil system operating throughout it. With Adam's sin, a pall of evil—a curse—fell on all matter— sun, moon, stars, earth, animals, vegetation, and man.

Did this mean that God then had to change His original plans? No, because God is immutable—unchanging. God has no Plan B's, only Plan A's.

Concerning His purpose for restoring and retrieving His good creation from corruption, God announced to Satan that one day He would defeat him through the seed of a woman. (See Genesis 3:15.) God did not say to Satan, "Now that you have marred what I've made, I will eventually have to throw it all away!" What He said was, "You are a defeated foe, which I will one day prove before all creation!"

Earth is Eternal

Initially, Satan's evil system prospered and man became so base that God sent a flood which drowned every human being, except for the godly family of Noah. Even here God did not destroy creation, rather He set the sign of the rainbow in the sky saying,

> "This is the sign of the covenant which I make between Me and you, and every living creature that is with you, for perpetual generations: I set My rainbow in the cloud, and it shall be for the sign of the covenant between Me and the earth. It shall be, when I bring a cloud over the earth, that the rainbow shall be seen in the cloud; and I will remember My covenant which is between Me and you and every living creature of all flesh; the waters shall never again become a flood to destroy all flesh. The rainbow shall be in the cloud, and I will look on it to remember the everlasting covenant between God and every living creature of all flesh that is on the earth."(Genesis 9:12-16, NKJV)

Eventually, Jesus, the Word of God, was conceived in a virgin by the Holy Spirit. At age thirty-three, He took up His divine mission and went to the cross to shed His blood as payment for the rebellion of God's prize man. This was based on the eternal and divine principle that says, "Without shedding of blood there is no remission of sin." (Hebrews 9:22, NKJV).

Rebellion against God was a violation of the highest order that demanded payment. The violated God became himself that payment. As the payment, He defeated Satan and restated His legal rights to evict Satan from His good creation. This brings us to the present age, where God is continuing to add men to His kingdom, while Satan continues to operate his evil system, for a limited time and within certain boundaries.

With this background, let us now return to Malachi and read:

Behold, I will send you Elijah the prophet before the coming of the great and dreadful day of the Lord. And he will turn the hearts of the fathers to the children, and the hearts of the children to their fathers, lest I come and strike the earth with a curse." (Malachi 4:5-6, NKJV)

A Great Spiritual Awakening

It has never been God's intention to condemn what He has made. He does not want the earth to die under the curse of evil. To avoid the death of creation, God is sending Jesus to fully evict Satan's system along with all the people involved in his evil. Before Jesus arrives, however, Elijah the prophet will come from the courts of heaven to bring about a great spiritual awakening. With

Elijah's ministry, hearts are going to change. "...he will turn the hearts of the fathers to the children, and the hearts of the children to their fathers." (Malachi 4:6, NKJV). Elijah's ministry is going to touch the wayward heart of Israel and the nations. He will invade the perverse thinking that calls evil good and good evil. He is going to challenge immoral, selfish, money-mad, career-bound parents, and rebellious, selfish, immoral children. He is going to strike at the heart of rebellion against the authority of the Kingdom of God. Families are going to be united in Jesus, as Elijah ministers under the anointing of the Holy Spirit. Transformed hearts will result in transformed families, just as John the Baptist brought about in Israel prior to the appearance of Jesus.

John The Baptist

Zacharias was an aged priest in Israel. One day as he performed his duties in the temple an angel appeared to him and announced that he and his wife would have a son who would be "...great in the sight of the Lord,....He shall also go before Him in the spirit and power of Elijah, 'to turn the hearts of the fathers to the children,' and the disobedient to the wisdom of the just; to make ready a people prepared for the Lord." (Luke 1:15, 17).

Matthew records that this is exactly what John did when he became a young man:

> In those days John the Baptist came preaching in the wilderness of Judea and saying, "Repent for the kingdom of heaven is at hand!" For this is he who was spoken of by the prophet Isaiah, saying: "The voice of one crying in the wilderness: 'Prepare the way of the Lord; make His paths straight.' " (Matthew 3:1-3, NKJV)

Revival broke out under John's ministry. Scores thronged daily to his services. Many in Israel were baptized in the Jordan River, "confessing their sins." There was revival among God's covenant people. Revival is for the Church. It produces bold, effective witnesses in the world. The revival of John also brought the religious leaders, debaters of the law, and traditionalists out to hear a fresh message. What they received was an unsophisticated rebuke and call for genuine change. Because of the gravity of Church leadership, revival always calls for a purging in the pulpit as well as in classrooms of scriptural scholarship. Revival addresses everybody. No one is exempt from a visitation of God. John addressed the ordinary believer, he addressed the religious leaders and he made both aware of the first and Second Coming of Messiah.

John said, "...he that cometh after me is mightier than I...he shall baptize you with the Holy Ghost and with fire...And he will thoroughly purge his floor, and gather his wheat into the garner; but he will burn up the chaff with unquenchable fire." (Matthew 3:11-12). This Jesus did not do at His first coming. Jesus did not burn up evil people and destroy their roots with fire in the first advent. The earth has not been purged of evil, as of this moment. Only the legal rights to evict the evil system was obtained at the cross. Jesus will come a second time to complete the fiery cleansing spoken of by John. Therefore, when Malachi said, "...the day cometh that shall burn as an oven," he was speaking of Christ's second coming—which will be preceded by the return of Elijah. As John the Baptist's ministry was in Judah so will Elijah's ministry by based there.

The Two Witnesses

In Revelation 11, we find a description of two prophets who will come from the courts of heaven in the final days of human history. Their ministry will last three and one-half years. During this period of time great signs and wonders will be done by them. Revelation 11:3 calls them "two witnesses," prophets who will dress in the ancient garb of sackcloth, as the Old Testament prophets did.

The identity of the two witnesses has always been a subject for discussion, but Scripture gives us several guideposts. Zechariah 4:11-14 symbolizes the two witnesses as the "two olive trees" and the "two candlesticks" which stand in the presence of the Lord. Since Zechariah prophesied this 500 years before the birth of Jesus, we know the two witnesses are Old Testament prophets. These two prophets have been standing in the presence of God for nearly 3,000 years. We can only imagine the glory these men will exude, as they walk about Israel under orders from heaven. Moses' face had shoots of blinding light radiating from it after he had spent only a few hours in God's manifest presence. Elijah and his companion witness have been ministering at the very throne of glory for thousands of years. Without doubt, the glory we attribute to angels will also saturate these witnesses. For the meek, their presence will be astounding, but for the rebellious, they will be greatly annoying. No mortal will even hold a candle to their power over man and nature.

That Elijah is one of these two witnesses is clear from Malachi's prophecy, *"Behold I send you Elijah the prophet before the coming of the great and dreadful day of the Lord."* Elijah's coming is not a metaphor. Malachi said clearly, "I send you Elijah." Devout Jews have always taken it literally and there is no reason for the Church to do otherwise. As to the second witness, since it is appointed unto man to die once (Hebrews 9:27), and Elijah and Enoch were two key prophets who never died, some scholars suggest Enoch may possibly be the second witness with Elijah. They maintain this position in view of the fact that the two witnesses will be killed after three-and-one-half years of ministry. (See Revelation 11:7-8.)

Yet, the miracles the "two witnesses" will perform look much like the ministry of Moses in Egypt. And it was Moses and Elijah who met with Jesus on the Mount of Transfiguration where they all glistened in the glory of God. It, therefore, seems plausible to consider Moses as the second witness with Elijah.

The Ministry of the Two Witnesses

"And I will give power to my two witnesses, and they will prophesy one thousand two hundred and sixty days, clothed in sackcloth." These are the two olive trees and the two lampstands standing before the God of the earth. And if anyone wants to harm them, fire proceeds from their mouth and devours their enemies. And if anyone wants to harm them, he must be killed in this manner. These have power to shut heaven, so that no rain falls in the days of their prophecy; and they have power over waters to turn them to blood, and to strike the earth with all plagues, as often as they desire. When they finish their testimony, the beast that ascends out of the bottomless pit will make war against them, overcome them, and kill them. And their dead bodies will lie in the street of the great city which spiritually is called Sodom and Egypt, where also our Lord was crucified. Then those from the peoples, tribes, tongues, and nations will see their dead bodies, three-an-a-half days, and not allow their dead bodies to be put into graves. And those who dwell on the earth will rejoice over them, make merry, and send gifts to one another, because these two prophets tormented those who dwell on the earth. Now after the three-and-a-half days the breath of life from God entered them, and they stood on their feet, and great fear fell on those who saw them. And they heard a loud voice from heaven saying to them, "Come up here." And they ascended to heaven in a cloud, and their enemies saw them. In the same hour there was a great earthquake and a tenth of the city fell. In the earthquake seven thousand people were killed, and the rest were afraid and gave glory to the God of heaven. (Revelation 11:3-13 NKJV).

The subject of "last days" is historically unpopular. The world is always in a mess, yet we do not want to think of life as we know it coming to an end. Nevertheless, it is winding down. One day the system that drives our way of doing things will perform its final fireworks. One last loud explosion with a world leader known as the antichrist, and God's two witnesses will come from His courts to minister in and to Israel for three-and-a-half years. Then Jesus will return to earth to establish His kingdom.

Most eschatology gives considerable attention to the antichrist and the evil he will inflict upon men during the last days of human government. We need, however, to comfort the believers and Israel with the truth God has revealed in His Word about the Holy Spirit's ministry during the last days. Under the anointing of the Holy Spirit, God's two prophets are going to inflict tremendous hardship on Satan's man. The antichrist is going to override the Jews in Israel temporarily, but it will be a miserable victory and short-lived. News flashes will cover the earth as man looks on in shock over the sudden turn of events in the Middle East, when the power of the two witnesses begins to challenge the policies of the antichrist.

Elijah and his companion will have a mandate from God. Their ministry will be to help Israel when all nations have abandoned them, although their works will probably have world-wide effects. Supernaturally empowered, they will be unstoppable. "And if anyone wants to harm them, fire proceeds from their mouth and devours their enemies. And if anyone wants to harm them, he must be killed in this manner" (Revelation 11:5, NKJV). This means that whatever evil men plot against the two prophets will boomerang.

We have a precedent for such a scenario in the contest between Moses and Pharaoh. When Pharaoh's magicians copied Moses and turned their rods into serpents, Moses' rod swallowed theirs. Each time Pharaoh hardened his heart or threatened Moses, Pharaoh's predicament only worsened. God working through His people is greater than Satan working through his emissaries. Each time Moses went to Pharaoh for the release of God's people, and was refused, plagues and diseases fell on Egypt while Israel was protected. When darkness fell on Egypt so that men cried out in pain, Israel had light in Goshen.

Revelation says of the two witnesses, "These have power to shut heaven, so that no rain falls in the days of their prophecy; and they have power over waters to turn them to blood, and to strike the earth with all plagues, as often as they desire." (Revelation 11:6, NKJV). During his ministry in Israel under wicked King Ahab, Elijah once shut up the heavens so that it did not rain for three years. Queen Jezebel took royal troops and sent them looking everywhere for Elijah so that she might have him killed, but he escaped. This tells us that God's man walking in God's plan is unkillable, until God has finished with His plan. This should encourage the Church today to stand up and get on with the business of God, regardless of the opposition.

After three-and-half years, Elijah and his companion will have completed their work, and they will be killed. Their bodies will lie in the streets of Jerusalem for three-and-a-half days. In the perverted mind-set of the ungodly, the death of the godly will be seen as such a blessing that they will send gifts to each other. The whole world will celebrate the scene. No doubt it will be covered on world-wide television.

> Then those from the peoples, tribes, tongues, and nations will see their dead bodies three-and-a-half days, and not allow their dead bodies to be put into graves. And those who dwell on the earth will rejoice over them, make merry, and send gifts to one another, because these two prophets tormented those who dwell on the earth." (Revelation   11:9-10, NKJV)

What a picture of the unredeemable quality of this world system. There is no reversing the downward spiral of the anti-God society of the last days. This is why we work. Many in the world can be rescued but the system will die, as it should. Jesus said, "Work while it is day for the night cometh when no man can work." The world is growing dark. Comparatively speaking, few will be saved in the last hours, because of the hardness of men's hearts. When people celebrate the death of the righteous, it is the midnight of civilization. Human nature has fully decayed when ungodliness executes righteousness.

But look what happens next. After three-and-a-half days, the two prophets will arise in front of the world's cameras and "great fear" will grip the world. Antichrist will be put on the run. Evil will be in disarray. Fighting will ensue at Armageddon, and the Son of God will appear with an innumerable host of saints and angels. With laser-like words coming from His mouth, the great world-class, political wizard, antichrist, will be plunged into hell. War will cease. Israel will be delivered from Gentile oppression. And the earth will settle down underthe wings of Jesus for a thousand years of healing and prosperity.

My admonition to Israel is this: when the World turns against you, turn to God. He has guaranteed your deliverance. "When you are in distress, and all these things come upon you in the latter days, when you turn to the Lord your God and obey His voice (for the Lord your God is a merciful God), He will not forsake you nor destroy you, nor forget the covenant of your fathers which He swore to them (Deuteronomy 4:30-31).

My admonition to the Church is this: Stop trying to recreate the renaissance Church of pomp and pageantry and let us get down to the business of preparing the way for the King. Both Joel (Joel 2:28-29) and Luke (Acts 2:17-18), tell us clearly that the Holy Spirit will be poured out in the closing days of human history. With the Holy Spirit there will be signs and wonders in nature, and the displays will be powerful in dimension. There will be spiritual manifestations among believers in the form of God-birthed visions, dreams, and abundant prophecy. Prophecy is a sign from God. Before the Lord returns to earth it will become commonplace in the Church. Men, women, servants, and handmaidens—that is ordinary laymen—will be prophesying. The supernatural stirrings in the Church today are but a foretaste of the coming outpourings of the Spirit in preparation for our Lord's return. Let us be open to His unfolding plans as His Spirit increasingly manifests himself among us.